Mark Ablett is a barrister specialising in the full spectrum of the consequences of relationship breakdown both in financial terms and where children are involved. He is frequently instructed in high value and complex financial cases and his abilities have been described as "way beyond his year of call". He is frequently published in journals and contributes to practitioner texts, as well as regularly giving seminars and running the Family Law Podcast, which is leading in its category.

A Practical Guide to Barder Events in Financial Remedy Proceedings in Family Law

A Practical Guide to Barder Events in Financial Remedy Proceedings in Family Law

Mark Ablett

Barrister, Pump Court Chambers

Law Brief Publishing

Published 2024 by Law Brief Publishing, an imprint of Law Brief Publishing Ltd
30 The Parks
Minehead
Somerset
TA24 8BT

www.lawbriefpublishing.com

Paperback: 978-1-916698-35-2

To my daughter, who tried her hardest
to stop me writing this book.

FOREWORD

In 2011 I appeared for the executors of the estate of a former client, a publican in his early 50s, who had died some 12.5 months after the making of a final financial remedy consent order. I was instructed to respond to an application by the deceased's former wife to set aside the final order, so that she could seek to recover all or part of his c£1m award, which had been funded largely from her non-marital wealth. The application was founded on the publican's death being a *Barder* event.

The set aside hearing was listed before Mr Justice Mostyn. Appearing in front of his Lordship was always enjoyable and rewarding but also challenging and unpredictable. On this occasion his Lordship swept into court and before the wife's counsel could say a single word Mostyn J said "*it's not a supervening event is it? Death, it's going to happen to all of us....*" Somewhat taken aback, the wife's counsel hurriedly reminded him of a number of cases including *Smith* and *Reid* which seemed to have settled the position that an unexpected death could be a *Barder* event. His Lordship was not only unmoved but reeled off the statistics for the percentage of men of the husband's age who would be likely to die during the next year.

Not surprisingly, after that unexpected start to the hearing, the wife's application was dismissed both on the basis that the husband's death was not unforeseeable but that 12.5 months was too long after the final order to comply with *Barder.* The decision was not reported. If it had been, it would almost certainly have been included by Mark in this remarkably helpful book. Certainly, if this book had been available to me then, it would have been a hugely valuable resource for preparing for that application.

The facts in *Barder* are truly shocking and, as Mark rightly observes, we should not forget the human tragedy in the background. Perhaps it is trite to observe that without such an unexpected and appalling event this area of law may never have developed, or at least not until such a fundamentally altering event arose in a different case. The advent of the Matrimonial Proceedings and Property Act 1970 and the Matrimonial Causes Act 1973 significantly increased the level of matrimonial finance awards, not least because the court had by then acquired the power to make property adjustment orders. Yet, until the decision in *Barder* in 1988, there was no mechanism for setting aside an order due to a subsequent event. It is now an established form of relief and will, no doubt, continue to be developed and enhanced.

The relationship between *Barder* applications and the *Thwaite* jurisdiction has been complicated and, at times, confused. This book not only comprehensively sets out the development timeline for both areas but succinctly summarises the conditions that presently apply to these distinct applications. As the introduction of r9.9A and PD9A of the Family Procedure Rules have also bought clarity to the application process, this book provides an excellent resource for any practitioner where events after the final order may have led to it being unfair.

We will see in time whether the retirement of Mr Justice Mostyn leads to a slowing of the development of financial remedies law without his turbo-powered output to propel it. Whatever happens in future this is certainly an appropriate time to review the law in these discreet but fundamentally important areas.

Edward Boydell KC
May 2024

PREFACE

This book is an attempt to bring some order and certainty to the Barder jurisdiction, and in default of that aim, to be at the very least a helpful compendium of the most relevant cases, categorised and summarised in a manner intended to assist the practitioner. That there are more failed than successful attempts at Barder appeals (or now set asides) says everything about the exceptionalism required for this jurisdiction to be invoked. The fact that Covid did not spark a successful Barder set aside may surprise some. The case law suggests that in part that was down to the way some of the applications were made. It is hoped that we do not have to deal with a similar catastrophic event in the near future, as even the silver lining of yet more case law will do little to cheer us up.

Recently, the sheer existence of the Barder jurisdiction has been questioned in light of the Supreme Court's judgment in *Unger and another (in substitution for Hasan) v Ul-Hasan (deceased) and another* [2023] UKSC 22, if only because on the face it, the jurisdiction could be seen as incompatible with the judgment in that case. In also considering the somewhat analogous jurisdiction from Thwaite, the judicial railing against the breadth of interpretation of these jurisdictions is exposed. It may be with the retirement of Mostyn J that Thwaite in particular is safe for now (Barder as a concept having been codified in the FPR), but as with any equitable jurisdiction, the precise test and the precise jurisdiction will always be tested and questioned. It is why I have sought to compile the various dicta and wranglings throughout the authorities into one definitive checklist of considerations when making a Barder application. This is not through any inflated sense of self-importance, more from the fact that I felt it would be remiss not to, having gone through so many cases, each of which add their own gloss and interpretation.

I have inevitably not covered every base nor mentioned every case. It is intended to be a helpful guide and not a tome with which to prop up your computer monitor. I do hope it proves to be more the former than the latter.

I lastly wish to record my thanks to Edward Boydell KC, not only for his wonderful foreword but also for his guidance and input.

The law should be considered accurate as at 25 April 2024.

Mark Ablett
May 2024

CONTENTS

INTRODUCTION

A final order in financial remedy proceedings is final, subject to those elements which are variable under the Matrimonial Causes Act 1973. Yet, the finality of such orders is potentially vulnerable by virtue of subsequent events, be it the discovery of material non-disclosure or, for the purposes of this book, an event or development so significant that it changes the fundamental basis on which the order was based. The latter, in a nutshell, is a Barder event.

This book will start from the beginning, considering the seminal case of *Barder v Barder (Caluori Intervening)* [1987] 2 FLR 480 before tracing the evolution of the principle through case law up to 2023, as well as considering the quasi-analogous jurisdiction stemming from the Court of Appeal's judgment in *Thwaite v Thwaite* [1981] 2 FLR 280 and the judicial challenges to that jurisdiction. A brief glance will also be cast in the direction of *Unger and another (in substitution for Hasan) v Ul-Hasan (deceased) and another* [2023] UKSC 22, which deals with some of the technical justifications for the existence of the *Barder* jurisdiction in cases of a party's death. Chapters are based on event themes running through the case law but invariably not every form of attempted *Barder* event will be analysed.

The book will conclude with an outline of the procedure to be followed in such an eventuality and practical considerations such as costs, together with a proposed definitive list of *Barder* conditions drawn from the case law analysed in this book.

It is hoped by the end of this book, readers will have a better understanding of what is likely to constitute a *Barder* event and will be accordingly forearmed if such a scenario arises in practice. It will inevitably be the exception not the norm and the case law is marked more by unsuccessful attempts than successful applications.

For the sake of ease throughout this book, the parties in cases discussed will be referred to generally by the anonymous abbreviation of 'W' and 'H' or 'M' and 'F'. No disrespect is intended to any of these litigants who after all, we have to thank for the body of case law on which we rely.

CHAPTER ONE

CONTEXT

Before considering *Barder* itself, it must be put in context. Section 31F(3) of the Matrimonial and Family Proceedings Act 1984 states: "*Every judgment and order of the family court is, except as provided by this or any other Act or by rules of court, final and conclusive between the parties.*" A final order is supposed to be final and consistent with the rule in *Henderson v Henderson* (1843) 67 ER 313, should dispose of all relevant matters of dispute between the parties.

There are however, various ways in which a final order may be challenged (excluding the court's *Barrell* jurisdiction):

a. Variation under section 31 Matrimonial Causes Act 1973

b. A conventional appeal on the basis that the decision was wrong in law or procedurally unjust.

c. An appeal out of time on the basis of a *Barder* event.

d. Set aside for fraud or mistake.

e. Set aside for material non-disclosure (which does not have to be fraudulent in nature)

f. Variation or discharge of undertakings within an order

g. Variation or set aside under the *Thwaite* jurisdiction.

Some of these routes allow the entire order to be challenged. Others, for example variation, are limited to certain aspects of the order such as periodical payments, an order for lump sums by instalments or the mechanics of an order for sale of property.

Authority for these routes is almost entirely found in black letter law. The so-called traditional routes of set aside (items (c), (d) and (e) above) are set out in paragraph 13 of practice direction 9A Family Procedure Rules. In the wording of paragraph 13.5 PD9A, a *Barder* event is characterised as "*a subsequent event, unforeseen and unforeseeable at the time the order was made, which invalidates the basis on which the order was made.*"

None of these routes should be taken lightly and inevitably they will carry costs risks; even variation proceedings which fall within the no order principle are specifically marked out in paragraph 4.4 practice direction 28A Family Procedure Rules for consideration as to the parties' conduct in the circumstances of the case.

As will emerge through the consideration of the various case law, *Barder* applications should be seen as a last resort. It is why context is important; if more conventional routes of challenge to an order exist, they should be explored before the somewhat nuclear option of the *Barder* set aside.

CHAPTER TWO

BARDER V BARDER (CALUORI INTERVENING)

So, to the originating authority. In 1973, David and Christina Barder married. They had two children in 1976 and 1978 but the marriage did not last. In July 1983, David left the family home and Christina remained with the children. On 25 September 1984, Mr and Mrs Barder were granted their Decree Absolute on Christina's undefended adultery petition.

Ancillary relief proceedings, as they were then called, followed and in the heady surrounds of Basingstoke County Court in February 1985, they settled their dispute with a consent order. This was duly approved by Mr Registrar Fuller. The essential provision was that H would transfer to W all his interest in the family home with W undertaking to redeem the mortgages and H would pay substantial periodical payments for the benefit of the children.

On 25 March 1985, the unthinkable happened; W killed both children and then herself. The unimaginable position in which H found himself should not be overlooked notwithstanding that the law tends to focus on the procedure and the technical rather than the human. At the centre of this case and of many subsequent cases in this line of authorities is appalling heartache and tragedy.

The order remained executory, as in it was yet to be implemented and the time for appeal had expired a month earlier (it was then just 5 days). On 23 April 1985, H issued a notice seeking leave to appeal out of time against the order. For the purposes of this book, the key plank on which the appeal rested was that if the order remained unchanged, the property would be disposed of in accordance with W's testamentary wishes and her mother would be the sole beneficiary. In other words, if the order remained unchanged, H would have nothing from the family home and W's mother would have everything. As H pleaded, W's death and the children's death fundamentally altered the basis upon which the order was made and the Matrimonial Causes Act was not intended to make provision for W's mother.

W's mother, Jacqueline Caluori, was given leave to intervene on 18 September 1985 and on 15 November 1985, H was given leave to appeal and succeeded, with the appeal being allowed and the order being set aside. The original judgment was on the basis of vitiation by fundamental mistake.

Mrs Caluori successfully appealed (2:1) to the Court of Appeal and H then appealed to the House of Lords.

The appeal in the Court of Appeal was framed around three questions, and this approach was mirrored by Lord Brandon of Oakbrook in the House of Lords. The three questions were:

1. Whether W's death had caused the suit to abate, so that the county court judge had no jurisdiction to entertain the husband's application for leave to appeal out of time.

2. Whether, if there was jurisdiction, the judge was right to exercise his discretion to grant leave to appeal out of time.

3. Whether, if there was jurisdiction and if the judge was right to exercise his discretion to grant leave to appeal out of time, he was also right to allow the appeal.

Question 1 engages an interesting dichotomy which continues until this day, namely the interplay between the death of one party and the continuation of the suit which was considered recently by the Supreme Court in *Unger and another (in substitution for Hasan) v Ul-Hasan (deceased) and another* [2023] UKSC 22, which will be touched on below.

Back to *Barder*, the various wranglings of the Court of Appeal will not be set out.

Dealing with question 1, the intervener's case was that given W had died, the court had no jurisdiction to entertain an appeal; the only jurisdiction it had was to enforce the order on behalf of the intervener. Remarkably, a case dealing with this very point just a few years earlier, *Purse v Purse* [1981] Fam. 143, was not cited to the Court of Appeal in *Barder* but was considered by Lord Brandon in the House of Lords. In *Purse*, the Court of Appeal distinguished between the court's appellate function and the clear prohibition on the personal representative of a deceased party invoking the court's jurisdiction under the Matrimonial Causes Act on behalf of the estate, as set out in *Sugden v Sugden* [1957] P 120.

Lord Brandon agreed with the decision in *Purse*, albeit not all the reasons; he approved in particular of the judgment of Sir John Arnold P. His own journey through the authorities can be seen in the *Barder* judgment and will not be repeated here. He agreed however, with the distinction drawn in Purse, noting:

> "*The purpose of the statutory right of appeal is to enable decisions of a county court which are unjust to be set aside or varied by the Court of Appeal. The fulfilment of that purpose is not made any the less necessary or desirable by the death of one of the parties to the cause in which the decision was made. In a case other than a matrimonial cause I do not think that it would even be suggested that the statutory right of appeal would lapse because of the death of one of the parties to it. I cannot see why a matrimonial cause should be different in this respect.*"

It follows that the right to appeal out of time must survive the death of one of the parties to the suit. Lord Brandon also noted that the corollary of the intervener's case must be that the right survives; the intervener's case was that the court could enforce the order. It would not be right for that position to be immune to defeat, i.e. the court must be able to refuse to enforce the order and set aside the order in the same way as if W still lived.

Question 2 of course is much less theoretical and turns on the facts of the case. Of interest is that little weight was placed by Lord Brandon on the fact that the order was by consent. As has been subsequently confirmed in numerous cases such as *Sharland v Sharland* [2015] UKSC 60, the force of the agreement stems from the order as approved by the court, not the agreement as some form of contract.

Lord Brandon, in agreeing that leave to appeal should have been given, balanced the competing interests of finality in litigation and justice requiring cases to be decided on true facts, not assumptions which later are conclusively shown to have been erroneous. He tied together in effect questions 2 and 3; the merits of the substantive appeal go hand in hand with whether leave to appeal out of time should be granted.

He went on to set out the essential conditions which any *Barder* application must today satisfy, as follows:

1. New events have occurred since the making of the order which invalidate the basis, or fundamental assumption, upon which the order was made, so that, if leave to appeal out of time were to be given, the appeal would be certain, or very likely, to succeed.

2. The new events should have occurred within a relatively short time of the order having been made.

3. The application for leave to appeal out of time should be made reasonably promptly in the circumstances of the case.

4. The grant of leave to appeal out of time should not prejudice third parties who have acquired, in good faith and for valuable consideration, interests in property which is the subject matter of the relevant order.

Later authorities have added a fifth condition: namely that no alternative mainstream relief is available to the applicant which broadly remedies the unfairness caused by the new event. Later authorities have also confirmed that even if all 5 conditions are satisfied, there remains a discretion open to the court to refuse to set aside an order, albeit this will likely only apply where the original order was made by consent. These will be explored throughout this book and a conclusive test proposed at the conclusion.

Clearly the second condition can never be capable of complete prescription in terms of time, but Lord Brandon considered it unlikely that the time could be as much as a year and in most cases it will be no more than a few months.

The third condition reminds readers of the rather cold nature of the law. An application must be brought promptly, notwithstanding the fact that in this case, H was grieving the murder of his two children, if not necessarily the suicide of his ex-wife.

The fourth condition is in effect the equity's darling argument which crops up in various forms, for example as a defence to setting aside a disposition under s.37 Matrimonial Causes Act 1973.

Yet, it is the first condition which realistically dominates the authorities and the ongoing difficulty practitioners will have in conclusively advising their clients. What counts as a *Barder* event? And as will become clear, implicit within this is whether the event was foreseeable.

Certainly in *Barder*, the fact that the house was transferred to W can clearly be inferred to be for the purpose of providing her and the children with a home for the foreseeable future. That purpose ceased the moment W undertook her despicable act and so quite clearly, the basis of the order was undermined.

As will be seen later on this book, authorities have gone on to consider not just the nature of the events but the effect of an order. A distinction is drawn for example between an order which simply recognises each party's entitlement to their share of their assets, i.e. a sharing case versus a needs-based award where a party is getting more under the order than they would otherwise have. It is the latter specie of case which is generally susceptible to a *Barder* claim.

How is this different to Ul-Hasan?

Primarily because of the recentness of the decision, this book will briefly touch on the interplay between the House of Lords' decision in *Barder* and the Supreme Court's decision in *Ul-Hasan*, as referenced above.

In brief, *Ul-Hasan* concerned an application by the wife under Part III Matrimonial and Family Proceedings Act 1984 following a divorce in 2012 in Pakistan. Before the application could be finally determined, the husband died. W wished to continue her claim against H's estate. Mostyn J considered that he was bound by the Court of Appeal's decision in *Sugden v Sugden*, referenced above, but would otherwise have allowed W to continue her claim as he disagreed with the Court of Appeal. He granted a leapfrog appeal to W, hence the matter travelled directly to the Supreme Court.

W's appeal was unsuccessful. The Supreme Court was satisfied that a claim under the 1984 Act, as with a claim under the Matrimonial Causes Act 1973, is a personal right which can only be adjudicated between living parties. The claim cannot continue against the estate.

The Supreme Court approached the decision in line with Lord Brandon's three questions he posed in *Barder*, before going on to set out the essential conditions. Lord Brandon's first question as set out above is whether the court has jurisdiction at all; the question turns on the nature of proceedings.

To determine this, the court first had to consider, on their true construction, the relevant statutory provisions. If the 1973 and 1984 Act created personal rights and obligations which could only be adjudicated between living parties, that really was the end of the matter.

Mostyn J's analysis at first instance, in setting out his disagreement with the Court of Appeal in *Sugden*, rested on s.1(1) of the Law Reform (Miscellaneous Provisions) Act 1934, which provides for causes of action to continue against a person's estate after their death. The question then for the Supreme Court was whether the right to financial provision on divorce is or is not a cause of action which falls within s.1(1) of the 1934 Act.

As is set out in the Supreme Court's judgment from paragraph 40 onwards, there had already been numerous decisions setting out that the right to financial provision does not fall within s.1(1) of the 1934 Act.

The long line of case law will not be rehearsed but it is perhaps telling that 2 years after the Matrimonial Causes Act 1973, Parliament enacted the Inheritance (Provision for Family and Dependants) Act 1975; i.e. a specific route for dependants to claim from the estates of the deceased. It would arguably be unnecessary for this Act to be created in relation to bereaved spouses, particularly given the 'divorce fiction' under s.3(2) of the 1975 Act, if Parliamentary intention was for the rights created under the 1973 Act to survive one spouse's death. The one distinction is that the 1975 Act only bites if the deceased dies domiciled in England & Wales (thus less helpful to potential applications under Part III of the 1984 Act).

So in summary, at first blush the key difference between *Ul-Hasan* and *Barder* is on the first question addressed by both the Court of Appeal and the House of Lords in *Barder*, namely a question of jurisdiction. In *Barder*, the court was faced with an appeal, which is in effect a procedural entitlement clearly provided for by statute and procedure rules. It was not the pursuit of a discretionary order, a pursuit of a personal right, but merely the review of an order already made. This is quite clearly distinct from *Ul-Hasan*, in which W was seeking for the exercise of the court's discretion for financial relief notwithstanding the death of H.

However, as will be explored later on, there are *Barder* authorities where the court conducted a fresh review of an appropriate order on appeal, rather than simply reversing an order made, which was the case in *Barder*. The position is summarised by Lord Stephens at paragraph 100 of *Ul-Hasan*:

> "*If an applicant successfully satisfies the conditions for leave to appeal applying the principles in* Barder *and if the appeal is allowed, then the appeal court can, on a redetermination, consider what order ought to have been made, even though one of the spouses has died. I consider this to be a discrete but limited exception to the general rule that the 1973 Act creates personal rights and obligations which end with the death of a party to the marriage, and which cannot be pursued against the deceased's estate. I consider that this limited exception is not a sufficient basis on which to undertake a radical change to the construction of matrimonial legislation.*"

This seemingly unfair dichotomy, where the court can review a claim if one party dies just after an award, but a party cannot continue a claim if the other party dies just before an award, is the focus of Lord Leggatt's concurring judgment. It goes beyond the confines of this book to delve further and various subsequent articles have looked at how discrete the *Barder* exception really is to the general rule set out by Lord Stephens at paragraph 100.

CHAPTER THREE

A PARTY'S DEATH AS A BARDER EVENT

Death of a party is the most common *Barder* event and unsurprisingly so. Particularly where an award is needs-based, it is difficult to see on what basis those needs survive death. As will be seen in this chapter, there is a clear distinction between a sharing claim and a needs claim. The simple fact of death does not mean that someone should not have anything, that would be to ignore the concept of the marital acquest. Whilst a property being matrimonial does not mean for example that by default the beneficial interest in that property is shared equally, the basic concept of a standing entitlement to property in some form being an interest which should survive notwithstanding death is a simple enough concept.

Smith v Smith

Following relatively hot on the heels of *Barder* was *Smith v Smith* [1992] Fam 69. Marriage breakdown was in 1988 and W applied for ancillary relief in December of that year. The registrar quantified the total assets at approximately £107,000 and considered an equal division was the only fair result, so W was awarded a lump sum of £54k. In May 1989, W committed suicide, leaving her estate, which included the lump sum of course, to her daughter.

H appealed (as the procedure then was) on the basis of *Barder* and the appeal judge reassessed W's needs as those of the estate, namely her debts, and otherwise held they were non-existent. The lump sum was varied appropriately. The daughter appealed, successfully.

The Court of Appeal through Butler-Sloss LJ confirmed the correct approach is to consider what order should have been made with the knowledge that W only had approximately 6 months to live. It is this contradiction that vexed the appellant in *Ul-Hasan*; in *Smith* the court reconsidered the award, it re-exercised its statutory discretion, notwithstanding the fact that W had died.

Of course, this was a case that pre-dated *White v White* so the concept of the sharing principle as the base line did not formally exist (albeit readers of Lord Denning's family law judgments may disagree). The court considered the quantum of the lump sum balancing all the s.25 factors and, in what really is a precursor of the sharing principle, held:

> "*A wife with few or no needs, who had none the less made a significant contribution to the marriage, has, in my judgment, a right to recognition of that contribution in money terms where there are assets available to meet it, so long as the court does not act to the unjust detriment of the other spouse. He has an equal right to consideration of all the criteria under s. 25, with not only the past but, unlike the wife, his future resources and needs to be taken into account.*"

The appeal succeeded partially, in that the lump sum was varied downwards but to £25k.

It is noteworthy in this case that the structure of the original order dictated to an extent the outcome. In *Barder*, the deceased wife was the joint owner of the matrimonial home and so whilst the order was set aside under *Barder* (thus meaning H did not have to transfer his 50% share to W's estate), W's own 50% share of the home still would have passed to her estate if the tenancy had been severed (otherwise passing to H by survivorship). In *Smith*, the family home was in H's sole name, hence the registrar's order focused on needs and was structured as a lump sum. There was no pre-existing proprietary right of W's to preserve for the estate notwithstanding that the property was the matrimonial home. As will be seen a little later, the advent of sharing put paid to this potential injustice.

Barber v Barber

Just after *Smith* came *Barber v Barber* [1993] 1 FLR 476, which starts an interesting line of case law in relation to foreseeability of the new event, without really considering foreseeability itself. The parties had two children, age 16 and 10 and by court order they had, as was said at that time, joint custody with care and control to W and reasonable access to H. This changed when W became ill with liver disease and the children moved to live with H by agreement.

Financial remedy proceedings followed, with W seeking a property transfer order on the family home and H seeking an order for sale. After a contested hearing, the court ordered sale of the family home and division of the proceeds £125k to W, the balance to H with periodical payments to W of £5,500 pa. The medical evidence at the time was that W could expect to live at least another 5 years.

In fact, W died just three months later and H appealed, successfully. There appears in the judgment very limited consideration of the foreseeability of the event. After briefly summarising the medical evidence at final hearing, Glidewell LJ sets out:

"*The wife's death nullified the major reason for the property order made by Judge McKinney. It destroyed the basis upon which the order had been made. It was for that reason that the judge granted leave to appeal out of time.*"

The argument in this case turned much more on what to do next. The court confirmed the then fresh in the mind approach of Butler-Sloss LJ in *Smith*, namely to look at the case again armed with the knowledge that W would only live for 3 months. There would have been no property adjustment so W's half share as co-owner of the property would have passed to the two children. The court therefore allowed the appeal and awarded 40% of the family home to the children, in recognition of their mother's contribution to the marriage which they stood to inherit. The property would not be sold until the youngest child turned 18 or further order.

Richardson v Richardson

Richardson v Richardson [2011] 2 FLR 244 CA had two potential *Barder* events and is an example of a more complex structure to a decision requiring more complex analysis. It is also significant for the continuing conundrum arising from the decision in *Unger v Ul-Hasan* outlined in the previous chapter.

This was a long marriage of some 46 years, during which H and W ran a hotel business together as equal partners. The net assets were assessed on divorce as just under £11m, subject to one caveat. A few years prior to the divorce, a child had been seriously injured falling out of a hotel window, suffering brain damage. The potential damages owed to the child were not included as a liability on the asset schedule because both H and W believed their insurance would cover the claim.

At the final hearing, the only issue was the structure of an equal division. W received 47.5% of the assets in recognition of the fact that her award was dominated by cash whereas H's share was principally illiquid. W was to resign from the partnership which ran the hotel and H would indemnify her against all partnership liabilities; this duly took place shortly after the order was made.

As for the potential *Barder* events:

a. 6 weeks after the order was made, W died unexpectedly.

b. 12 weeks after the final order, H discovered that the insurer had avoided the policy.

It is noteworthy in relation to the latter that two of H's agents had been aware of the possibility of avoidance since before the final hearing but had not told H. The child was pursuing damages in court and was seeking over £3m; the insurance policy even if not avoided had a maximum limit of £2m.

H appealed out of time, saying W's death and the damages claim meant the award had to be reconsidered.

Dealing first with the death, H failed to overturn the award. This case serves as an important reminder that the simple fact of death does not immediately reopen an award. The death must invalidate the basis or fundamental assumption upon which the original order had been made, as set out by Lord Brandon in *Barder*. This case was a sharing case; W's award was nothing more than her equal share in the marital acquest. Why should her estate be deprived of what she rightfully earned during the marriage? One can see how the development of the law, in particular sharing, distinguishes the court's approach in this case versus for example the earlier case of *Smith*.

On the issue of the insurance claim, both had been aware of the claim, both could have explored the issue more thoroughly for example the level of cover available, which clearly was an issue regardless of avoidance by the insurer. It was described by Munby LJ as a "*known unknown*" and the court considered that due diligence would have uncovered the issue. It was not therefore a new event which undermined the original order nor was it that other vitiating factor of mistake.

However, the appeal did succeed slightly, because the court was satisfied that just because H's agent knew of the insurer's avoidance, did not mean H should be treated as equally aware. Munby LJ was satisfied that the insurance claim should be reflected somehow and he ordered that a forthcoming lump sum owed by H totalling £1.6m be varied so that he pays that sum less such sum (not exceeding £1m) representing 50% of any damages ordered to be paid and the costs incurred both in defending the action and making a claim against the insurer/broker. The structure of the order was varied so that £1m of the lump sum was initially paid into court. Note that the figure is £1m, i.e. 50% of £2m; it is the level the parties considered was covered by the policy.

The variation though must be seen in context. Munby LJ noted that, contrary seemingly to the estate's understanding, they were in fact a party to the insurance action. Munby LJ was satisfied that a successful claimant could claim against W's estate notwithstanding the indemnity and W's retirement from the partnership and that in fact W's estate was probably more vulnerable, being much more liquid than H's illiquid share of the assets.

The judgment finishes with a final word (or four paragraphs, to be precise) from Thorpe LJ, in which he noted:

> "*Cases in which a Barder event, as opposed to a vitiating factor, can be successfully argued are extremely rare, should be regarded by the specialist profession as exceedingly rare, and should not be thought to be extendable by ingenuity or the lowering of the judicially created bar.*"

The message, sent out in the context of an unsuccessful *Barder* appeal, was clear.

Reid v Reid

The fourth case considered sits between *Smith* and *Richardson*; *Reid v Reid* [2004] 1 FLR 736 and brings into further focus the question of foreseeability. It appears to be the first case post-*White* dealing with death as a *Barder* event.

W and H were married for 40 years. On divorce they reached agreement to sell the family home, where H was living, and divide the proceeds 60/40 in H's favour, which on sale would have led to £150k to H and £99k to W. W at the time already had her housing needs otherwise met, whereas H had to meet his from his share of the net proceeds. The division of the proceeds was contained in a recital to an order, which otherwise provided for dismissal of all claims.

Two months after the order confirming this agreed was made and 15 days after Decree Absolute, W died of a heart attack. During the course of proceedings, she had disclosed that she was registered blind, had high blood pressure and high cholesterol. She also had diabetes.

H issued a *Barder* application, seeking a variation to a 75/25 split in his favour, so a further £37k to him. This was on the basis that the fundamental assumption underlying the agreement and order had been invalidated by W's death. W's estate argued three points, each of which is of interest:

a. W's death, at age 74, was foreseeable so not a 'new' event.

b. Post *White v White*, W had a sharing/contributions claim which survived attack.

c. W had already received less than 50% of the assets because of H's needs so a further adjustment was unjustified.

Foreseeability will be touched on but, spoiler alert, H succeeded both in principle and in quantum; the estate was ordered to pay him a further £37k. In light of *Richardson* above, it would be interesting to see how a court would approach such a case today, bearing in mind the clear respect for a sharing case (it is why *Reid* is presented out of chronological order in this chapter). Of course, whilst *Reid* was post-*White*, it still preceded *Miller v Miller; McFarlane v McFarlane.*

On foreseeability, it was argued that the death of a woman at age 74 should have been recognised as an obvious likelihood at the time of the order; the fact that it happened sooner than perhaps expected was a matter of degree, rather than a new event. One could observe, arguing that death is always inevitable and that its timing does not make it a 'new event' would scupper this entire line of case law.

Counsel for H pointed to the fact that W had 13 years left to live per average life expectancy tables and that there was nothing disclosed in proceedings which pointed to W's imminent death.

Wilson J was not persuaded on foreseeability and the wording of his finding is significant for future cases:

> *"I find that the wife's death 2 months after the order was made was not reasonably foreseeable. Notwithstanding the possibility of death at any time, there was no material which should have placed the wife's death 2 months later into the minds of the parties as being a significant, ie more than a theoretical, possibility."*

The next argument was whether the new event undermined the basis of the order. Counsel for the estate made the kinds of arguments one would expect today, citing *White* in support of W having a share that should survive her death. Wilson J took the view that that this was very much a needs case and was persuaded by reference to the earlier case of *Smith*, which he considered sat comfortably with *White v White*. Again, one does wonder how Wilson J (as he then was) would approach judgment if he was hearing the same case today.

WA v Executors of the Estate of HA (deceased)

Turning to the case of *WA v Executors of the Estate of HA (deceased)* [2016] 1 FLR 1360. W was a wealthy heiress, with her assets mostly in trust. Whilst there was a pre-nuptial agreement in place, providing for no claims on divorce, it ultimately was not used (unsurprisingly post-*Radmacher v Granatino* [2010] UKSC 42). The family home (a £30m estate) was partly owned by a trust and was partly owned directly by W.

The parties separated in 2014 and it appeared to hit H very hard. Negotiations took place directly between solicitors and they reached an agreement as to a financial remedy to H. He was to receive £17.34m in two tranches, the first of which was immediately after the order was made and was duly paid.

22 days after the order was made, H committed suicide, leaving his estate to his three adult siblings (not the parties' three children). W applied to appeal out of time (as it still was then in 2015).

The appeal turned on two issues:

1. Was H's death foreseeable?

2. Was the structure of the award based on needs or sharing?

On point two, as made clear in *Richardson* a sharing award is not susceptible to challenge, whereas a needs-based award would be. There remained the question however, of what H's needs were on death, bearing in mind that the simple fact of death did not dis-entitle one to a needs award, per *Smith*.

Putting aside the issue of foreseeability, quite clearly in this case H's death undermined the fundamental assumption underlying the order. With inherited assets in trust, this was always going to be a needs-based award and the quantum of the lump sum was predicated on H having long-term housing and income needs.

The question of foreseeability is again interesting because of course if H's suicide was within the parties' contemplation at the time of the order, it was not a new event. The court was satisfied that whilst H was in a bad way, considering *Reid* above, H's suicide could not have been seen as a significant possibility by either the court or W. The court noted the simple fact that W agreed to pay him in excess of £17m demonstrated her lack of genuine awareness. The court followed *Reid* and adopted the test of whether there was a more than theoretical possibility of death.

In terms of a revised award, the court started with a sharing approach. Half of the matrimonial home (£15m) was owned directly by W and the court considered that was an asset to which the sharing principle applied, reflecting the joint contributions to married life. Reflecting W's sole financial contribution however, H was awarded 1/3, so £5m. Moor J was satisfied that such sum exceeded H's needs and so whilst the sharing award should not be reduced, it need not be added to in the way the original agreement provided for. The lump sum was therefore reduced to £5m and the estate had to repay W some £3.67m.

The judgment really is a touchstone for questions of foreseeability and the way to approach the quantum of a revised award in light of a *Barder* event being established.

Pensions

So established now is death as a potential ground to set aside an order that the latest raft of financial remedy precedent orders contain the following wording in relation to pensions:

i. "*there be the following consequential directions:*

(1) *it being agreed between the parties that in the event that the [respondent] / [applicant] non-member spouse predeceases the [applicant] / [respondent] member spouse after this order has taken effect but before its implementation the [applicant] / [respondent] member spouse shall [in order to prevent a loss of pension rights to the family overall] have the consent of the personal representatives of the [respondent] / [applicant] non-member spouse to apply to appeal out of time against the order under the Matrimonial Causes Act 1973, s 40A or s 40B (there being no requirement to obtain permission to apply to set aside an order under FPR 2010 r.9.9A).*"

The suitability for this clause to be used will depend on each case, for example if the pension is based on sharing or need, if it is a defined benefit pension or a defined contribution pension which will survive death, et cetera. The inclusion however, almost by default, in financial remedy orders recognises the relevance of death immediately proximate to a final order as fundamentally altering (at least potentially) the basis on which an order was made.

For a final dose of case law in this chapter, the recent case of *SY v Personal Representatives of the Estate of DY (Deceased)* [2023] EWFC 280 highlights the utility of the pension set aside clause, but also the danger (if the wording had been interpreted as total acceptance of the appeal/set aside without any replacement provision).

A pension sharing order of 14 September 2022 provided for pension sharing orders over H's two NHS pensions. W sadly passed away on 9 March 2023 and H sought to appeal out of time only the pension sharing order; Recorder Hames KC kindly disposed with the legal procedure which meant H should have sought a set aside from the same tribunal as the original order. W's estate conceded that the pension sharing orders should be set aside but sought in their stead a lump sum of some £51,480.51, being the pension lump sum the estate could receive if the pension sharing orders were not set aside. Recorder Hames KC was also persuaded that the *Barder* conditions were met; due to the lack of argument this was not explored in detail in the judgment.

There followed the familiar argument of needs versus sharing. H resisted the lump sum award on the basis that the pension sharing orders were premised on needs and in particular that they were viewed as future income rather than capital to be shared. Recorder Hames KC was unpersuaded. He noted that plainly a pension sharing award carries an element of sharing or entitlement and the fact that it was viewed as meeting future income needs did not change that. The lump sum was therefore ordered as a condition of the pension sharing orders being set aside. Whilst conceding an appeal in this case was common sense on behalf of the estate, they were deemed right and fair in pursuing the tangible loss to the estate as a result of the set aside.

CHAPTER FOUR

ECONOMIC CHANGE AS A BARDER EVENT

This chapter sits independently of the various cases in relation to Covid-19 as a *Barder* event, which forms the next chapter. Before the world had heard of Covid, litigants were arguing that economic change, both up and down, should be considered to be a *Barder* event.

When one negotiates an agreement or makes a submission to a judge, how much does the economic climate feature in the submission? At the time of writing, there is a cost-of-living crisis, energy bills are in a perilous state following Russia's invasion of Ukraine and the amount of interest one pays on a mortgage is sickening. Does that amount to a fundamental assumption which underlies an order or agreement? Possibly in relation to the quantum of spousal maintenance, possibly in relation to whether that maintenance order is index-linked. However, those orders are variable under s.31 Matrimonial Causes Act and needs-based and so if needs change, quantum can be varied. A jurisdiction already exists to remedy that wrong. At first blush, economic circumstances seem to be more a factor which would be reflected in the exercise of discretion, rather than a fundamental assumption.

The authorities in this chapter focus more on rapid change, particularly in terms of asset value. One can see the argument that if an agreement is premised on an asset being worth X but then within a short period of time due to unforeseen circumstances it becomes worth Y, that may well be an undermining feature. The scope of the authorities has been limited to post-*Barder* itself and is by no means exhaustive; this book would otherwise become a tome. A subsequent windfall in inheritance will be considered in a separate chapter.

Hope-Smith v Hope-Smith

Moving away from the rather grim topic of imminent death post-divorce, we turn to post-final order skulduggery. *Hope-Smith v Hope-Smith* [1989] 2 FLR 56 was the first post-*Barder* authority to involve leave to appeal out of time due to a change in the value of assets.

W and H divorced in 1985 after an 8-year marriage and on W's application, she was awarded a lump sum of £32k to be charged against the family home, with an order for sale in default if not paid within 28 days. H was the first one to apply for leave to appeal out of time and failed; the appellate judge dismissed the appeal and ordered the immediate sale of the house and payment to W from the net proceeds. At that time the house was worth £116k gross and the lump sum equated to 37.9% of the net equity (starting from the guide that existed at the time of the one-third rule).

As warned above, skulduggery from H ensued. In September 1986 W obtained a warrant for possession, but this was suspended until October 1987. In June 1988, W obtained leave to appeal out of time on the basis that the house was now worth £200k and sought an order which reflected the present value of the house, premised on the accompanying cost to her of rehousing later than intended.

The appeal was allowed. W hardly acted promptly, bearing in mind the *Barder* conditions, but this was excused given the delay was due to H's misconduct. The court did not consider that the original judge had acted wrongly because the original order sensibly provided for an enforcement mechanism. However, the court considered that the change in value was so significant that it did invalidate the basis on which the order was made and substituted an order for a percentage share of the net proceeds (40%), rather than a lump sum order; a useful judgment where any litigant seeks for an order to provide for lump sums rather than percentage division.

On the face of it, this authority suggests that the increase in gross value of an asset by 172% is sufficient to invalidate an order. This is of course a dangerous oversimplification, as the Court of Appeal set out in the next case of *Thompson*:

> *"We believe that percentages should be used with caution, for it is easy to see that a modest seeming percentage change in the figure for an asset or a liability may have a disproportionate practical effect on the order under appeal. Thus, if one posits that the principal asset of the former spouses is a house valued at £130,000, which is subject to a mortgage of £100,000, a rise of 30% or fall of 23% could wipe out or double the equity. We think it much better for the reviewing court, when considering questions of degree, to look in broad terms at the balance of the financial relationship created by the order under review, and then ask itself how this balance has been affected by the new state of affairs."*

More importantly, the decision in *Hope-Smith* is rooted in H's misconduct, more than anything else. The revised order in any event reflects the mischief of the original decision, just more fairly structured.

Thompson v Thompson

In *Thompson v Thompson* [1991] 2 FLR 530, the Court of Appeal was faced with an application for leave to appeal out of time, or rather an appeal from a Circuit Judge's dismissal of the same. H sold his business less than 2 weeks after the final order for more than twice the value adopted at final hearing; a jump from £20k to £45k.

The court concluded that, broadly speaking, the cause of the change in value did not matter for the purpose of considering whether the business sale was a new event, subject to 2 qualifications (albeit these were made clear not to be definitive statements of principle). Firstly, the change should not be the result of the deliberate misdeeds of the person who profits. Secondly, of course, is foreseeability.

The court was then posed with two considerations:

a. Was this the result of an erroneous valuation, was there a mistake, should someone have known about it?

b. Were there subsequent events which changed the value.

Quite clearly if it was a mistake which was possible to uncover by due diligence at the time of the final hearing, it is foreseeable and cannot be considered a new event.

The court in this case considered it was not reasonable to expect anyone at final hearing to have anticipated the jump in value, which was contrary to H's own pessimistic evidence on value. The court gave permission to appeal out of time against the original order and remitted the matter for re-hearing, in a rare case of not just substituting a new order.

Cornick v Cornick

The case of *Cornick v Cornick* [1994] 2 FLR 530 involves the happier occurrence of wild economic success post-divorce. Hearing the matter was a young judge called Mrs Justice Hale; whatever happened to her? This case remains the foundation for all *Barder* authorities in which economic change is pleaded as a supervening event and should be read in full by any contemplating an application on that basis.

In 1992, financial remedy proceedings took place before a District Judge on 18 December 1992 who awarded W a lump sum of £320k from the sale of the family home as well as £20,000 pa spousal periodical payments and £4,200 pa per child by way of child periodical payments.

The mathematics underlying the District Judge's decision were premised on the value of H's shares in the company of which he was deputy chairman. At the time of the hearing, the shares were worth £2.17 per share, making net assets (excluding share options which had not yet come due, and excluding pensions) of £649k, so W got 51% plus maintenance, or 36% including the share options.

By November 1993, the share price for H's shares had risen to £7.23, prompting W to make her application for leave to appeal out of time. This transformed the asset picture, with net assets (excluding share options and pensions) of £1,285,700, so a net effect of the original order of 26% to W.

By May 1995, the price had risen further, settling at £10.04 having peaked at £12.58 in February. This increased the net assets to £1,649,300 again excluding the share options and pensions, so a net effect of 20% to W. It is worth highlighting at this stage that in February 1991, the share price was £0.37.

Hale J warned herself against understandable sympathy to W. She postulated three different interpretations (which have formed the bedrock of future analysis of *Barder* events in this context):

1. A general change of circumstances – dismissed because the court has no power to vary capital settlements, which are intended to be final and are based upon a snapshot at the time of the trial.

2. The court made its decision on a mistaken basis, so significant that had it known the true facts it would have made a substantially different order. This is more akin to a material non-disclosure argument. W did not run mistake on appeal.

3. The change is a *Barder* event – it is on this that the court's discussion focused. Hale J characterised this as follows:

   "*Something unforeseen and unforeseeable had happened since the date of the hearing which has altered the value of the assets so dramatically as to bring about a substantial change in the balance of assets brought about by the order. Then, provided that the other three conditions are fulfilled,*

> *the Barder principle may apply. However, the circumstances in which this can happen are very few and far between. The case-law, taken as a whole, does not suggest that the natural processes of price fluctuation, whether in houses, shares or any other property, and however dramatic, fall within this principle."*

Hale J considered the case in point to fall within the general change of circumstances category and characterised W's case as simply saying it is all terribly unfair.

The key discussion was naturally whether a change in the value of assets known about and taken into account at the hearing, however dramatic, can amount to new events for the purposes of *Barder*. The point was taken that the change in value, what was termed a 'process over time' cannot amount to 'new events' and coming back to foreseeability, it is entirely foreseeable in theory that a share price might fluctuate.

However, in this case, Hale J was persuaded that the dramatic change was not something which could have been foreseen or put before the court on W's behalf at the hearing. But, the simple fact of unforeseeability is not enough to get home on a Barder application. Hale J was acutely conscious of a potential floodgates argument if a subsequent change in asset value was deemed sufficient to overturn an order and considered that consideration was fatal to W's application.

Thus in Hale J's judgment the case failed at the first limb of Lord Brandon's test. For completeness she considered the remaining limbs and found limb 2 and 3 fulfilled and limb 4 not relevant.

Of interest is the highlighting by Hale J of a general discretion notwithstanding the various tests. The court is not simply bound to set aside an order even if the various criteria are fulfilled. Referring to *Penrose v Penrose* [1994] 2 FLR 621 CA and the *per curiam* comments in that case, Hale J noted that the court has to consider whether W had any other, more appropriate, remedies to right any wrong. In this case, she continued to have the benefit of a periodical payments order and so she could easily have applied for a variation under section 31 Matrimonial Causes Act 1973. Hale J suggested a capitalised maintenance award (at that time not possible) as a logical solution and it is hard to disagree.

Myerson v Myerson (No 2)

Of course before Covid-19, there was one other dramatic economic event in recent memory; the financial crash of 2008. Enter the case of *Myerson v Myerson (No 2)* [2009] 2 FLR 147.

On 28 February 2008, Mr and Mrs Myerson settled their financial dispute at an FDR in front of Baron J. For reasons which will become clear, it is important that this was a consent order. The agreed division was a 57/43 split in H's favour, but the vast majority of H's share consisted of a substantial shareholding in a company called Principle Capital Holdings Ltd. By comparison, W's share consisted of £9.5m cash and a property worth £1.5m. W's lump sum was to be paid in bulk on 3 April 2008 with four instalments thereafter of £625k each year, so up to 3 April 2012.

The logic is clear; W received less than 50% but received the copper-bottomed assets. You may guess where this is going.

At the time of the FDR, the share price in PCH Ltd was £2.99. By the time the order was perfected on 19 March, the share price had fallen to £2.775. There followed a dramatic but not instantaneous fall; the share price held up largely until July 2008. On 4 November, the share price was £1.40, by 23 December 2008, the share price was £0.725 and by the date of the Court of Appeal hearing (11.03.2009), the share price was £0.275.

H brought an application to vary (not set aside) on 4 November. This case name is incidentally also authority for the fact that an FDR judge cannot subsequently conduct litigation, with H's applications having initially been brought before Baron J. It was not until 23 December that H made his application to appeal the consent order. By the point of the application, because of the drop in the share price, the asset split equated to 86/14 in W's favour. By the point of the supplemental skeleton argument advanced on H's behalf in the Court of Appeal, the division was 105.2/-5.2 in W's favour.

Interestingly, a trend of sufficient change warranting intervention sought to be identified in the authorities by H's counsel, effectively suggesting the authorities showed there was a threshold after which change would be sufficient. The one problem was *Cornick*, which was submitted (boldly) to be an outlier.

W's counsel, Nicholas Mostyn QC, made all the points one would expect and relied on *Cornick*. Thorpe LJ largely agreed with him. Again the floodgates arguments were noted and the points made by Hale J in *Cornick* repeated, but Thorpe LJ went further. He flagged specifically that this order was by consent; H agreed to this asset division and as submitted by W's counsel, shares may plummet but they may also soar and H had publicly issued bullish statements about the company's performance. Thorpe LJ was also unimpressed by H's position being that he would seek repayment of some of the £7m he had already paid W in exchange for an unspecified share in the company.

Thorpe LJ therefore granted permission but dismissed the appeal. Whilst the idea of identifying a trend of significance of change leading to orders being overturned is conceptually simple and has the benefit of providing some lodestone to work against, such submission did not find favour. *Cornick* is much more likely to be the reference point and in particular the three scenarios suggested by Hale J therein.

A couple of concluding observations in Thorpe LJ's judgment are worth highlighting:

a. On the issue of new events, something flagged and discussed in *Cornick*, Thorpe LJ was not satisfied that Lord Brandon's first condition demands some concrete event like the liquidation of a company. He held: "*Events in this context embrace happenings, developments or occurrences.*"

b. Thorpe LJ echoed the words of Hale J: "*the natural processes of price fluctuation, whether in houses, shares, or any other property, and however dramatic, do not satisfy the Barder test.*"

<u>Is the ability to vary a lump sum by instalments really an alternative jurisdiction?</u>

In the above cases the availability of an alternative jurisdiction to vary under s.31 Matrimonial Causes Act 173 was noted. Indeed it was because of this jurisdiction in relation to lump sums by instalments that specifically in relation to the outstanding lump sums due in *Myerson v Myerson*, Thorpe LJ considered H's appeal would have most uncertain prospects of success.

Periodical payments are of course variable and the considerations are familiar. Less common is the variation of a lump sum order by instalments and in respect of quantum is vanishingly rare. As to the court's approach, in *Westbury v Sampson* [2002] 1 FLR 166, Bodey J held:

> "*(58) The reopening under section 31 of the overall quantum of lump sum orders by instalments, especially when made as part of a package intended to be final (and all the more so when ordered by consent following an agreement) should only be countenanced when the anticipated circumstances have changed very significantly, and/or for cogent reasons rendering it quite unjust or impracticable to hold the payer to the overall quantum of the order originally made.*
>
> *(59) This formulation gives a little more latitude as regards section 31 of the Matrimonial Causes Act 1973 than do the*

> *Barder conditions for the grant of leave to appeal out of time; but that must, I think, follow from the statutory requirements under section 31(7) that the court is to consider all the circumstances."*

This was endorsed by Thorpe LJ in *Shaw v Shaw* [2002] 2 FLR 1204.

It has more recently been addressed by Mostyn J in *BT v CU* [2021] EWFC 87, an authority which crops up later in this book both as a Covid-19 authority and a statement of Mostyn J's views on the *Thwaite* jurisdiction. For the purposes of this section, Mostyn J's views on multiple lump sums is highlighted. He undertook a true to form trawl through the Law Commission's report of 1969 which was the bedrock for the Matrimonial Causes Act 1973. He pointed to the oddity of being able to have a series of lump sums which is in theory non-variable but a lump sum by instalments which is variable.

Mostyn J considered that if it looks like a lump sum spread over time then it probably is and should be considered a lump sum by instalments. Having reviewed the Law Commission's recommendations for s.31 Matrimonial Causes Act 1973 and having dismissed the only authority where the quantum of the lump sums had been varied (*Tilley v Tilley* (1980) 10 Fam Law 89), Mostyn J held:

> *"In my judgment, notwithstanding that the order in this case is to be characterised as a lump sum payable by instalments, it is not variable as to overall quantum under s. 31 Matrimonial Causes Act 1973. The overall quantum can only be set aside or altered under the Barder doctrine. Under s. 31 all that can be achieved is recalibration of the payment schedule."*

Mostyn J goes on to consider that s.31 did not in *BT v CU* give rise to a realistic alternative jurisdiction. The writer would agree. One can query whether the technical jurisdictional possibility of varying a lump sum order by instalments really amounts to a *Penrose v Penrose* alternative jurisdiction to be explored instead of a *prima facie* meritorious *Barder* claim.

The Court of Appeal is yet to consider Mostyn J's views but as things stand, it is difficult to see, where quantum is in issue, that a *Barder* application should fail the *Penrose* condition because of the existence of s.31 Matrimonial Causes Act 1973 in respect to lump sums.

CHAPTER FIVE

COVID-19 AS A BARDER EVENT

BT v CU (chapter 4) will form the concluding case in this section as, for the sake of judging any development in judicial attitude, the relevant cases will be taken in chronological order. It should be stated quite clearly that the chances of any *Barder* application being successfully made at the time of writing reliant on Covid-19 are slim to none. Whilst it is very much hoped that similar events will not plague us in the future, a pessimist imagines there will be future events which, even if not directly comparable to the Covid-19 pandemic, may at the very least be analogous. The reference in the following cases to *Myerson* are testament to that.

FRB v DCA (No 3)

First was *FRB v DCA (No 3)* [2020] EWHC 3696 (Fam), before Cohen J. The final hearing took place for three weeks in January and February 2020. Judgment was circulated in draft on 28 February 2020 and formally handed down on 30 March 2020 after a short hearing on 27 March 2020. For those who have tried to forget, the UK went into lockdown on 23 March 2020.

The final order, which was dated 27 March 2020, provided for W to be transferred the FMH mortgage free (£15 million) and a lump sum by instalments totalling £49 million. The timing of the lump sum instalments was based on dates volunteered by H during the hearing.

At the hearing on 27 March 2020, H's counsel informally (and presciently) invited the judge to delay handing down judgment on the basis that the then nascent pandemic was likely to have such an economic effect that the basis of the order was likely to be fundamentally undermined. He sought an adjournment until September 2020. This informal application was refused.

H appealed the order in a conventional sense, but permission was refused by the Court of Appeal. H's response was not to pay a penny of the lump sums due.

Two days before the first instalment of the lump sum was due, H applied to vary the lump sum order in timing and quantum. The application was framed in the alternative; either a variation under s.31 Matrimonial Causes Act 1973 or a set aside as a *Barder* application.

Unsurprisingly, H's application was premised on his claim that his assets had been drastically affected by the pandemic. He claimed an enormous reduction in his financial worth albeit he was unable to fully quantify that reduction. Pausing here; the lack of detail seems a bold admission to make. Cohen J noted the same thing; his statement scarcely touched on the assets which Cohen J had found were part of his assets at the final hearing. Instead he mentioned three listed companies, one of which had only dropped in value by 5%. H invited the court to undertake a wholesale revaluation exercise which would cost between £300-400k and would take 6 months.

Cohen J touches on the ability to vary the quantum of lump sums and his views align with Mostyn J's views set out in the previous chapter in *BT v CU.*

As for the *Barder* application, Cohen J was faced with H's proposed re-valuation exercise or a more summary approach. Cohen J considered that he could not take general judicial notice of a change on macro-economic grounds. The burden was on H to provide *prima facie* evidence of the change on which he relied. The utter lack of detail provided by H in the circumstances counted severely against him and his application was dismissed, albeit Cohen J accepted H may be able to argue for a recalibration of the timing of the lump sums.

This is less an authority akin to *Myerson* or *Cornick* as to whether Covid-19 constituted a *Barder* event and more a helpful lesson in how not to make a *Barder* application.

HW v WW

Next comes the judgment of HHJ Kloss in *HH v WW* [2021] EWFC B20, with some inventive anonymisation initials. The judgment is brilliantly clear and opens with: "*Is the Covid 19 pandemic and its impact upon the value of a key asset a sufficient ground to set aside a financial remedy consent order?*"

The short answer is yes in principle, but not in this case.

Like with *FRB v DCA*, this case was finalised on the cusp of the pandemic. The FDR took place on 12 March 2020. For context, Italy had already imposed a national quarantine on 9 March 2020.

The agreement between the parties provided for a series of lump sums (not by instalments) totalling £1 million, the first lump sum of £750k payable by 10 June 2020. The first lump sum was to be used to discharge the mortgage on the FMH which W would then retain. Like *Myerson*, H would retain the business. The overall deal saw W with 39.8% of the capital assets but again the rationale was clear; she was keeping copper-bottomed assets. As in *Myerson*, HHJ Kloss observed that no one forced either party into this deal and in particular the specific structure.

On 5 June, H applied to stay the lump sum order for 12 months. H did not pay the lump sum, W applied to enforce and approximately 2 weeks after W's enforcement application H applied to set aside the entire order. H relied on the alleged substantial change in the value of shares in the family company and the impact of the pandemic on his ability to pay the lump sum. All three applications came before HHJ Kloss, albeit the stay application was dismissed by consent due to having been overtaken by the *Barder* application.

It was accepted that were the *Barder* application to succeed, the case would in effect start afresh. New valuation evidence would be required and updated disclosure ordered.

In considering the law, HHJ Kloss referred to *Cornick* and *Myerson*. He refers also to *DB v DLJ* [2016] EWHC 324 (Fam), a judgment of Mostyn J in an application to show cause why the wife should not be held to the terms of an arbitral award. The judgment is not a *Barder* case but contains a helpful analysis of foreseeability starting at paragraph 36. HHJ Kloss cites two passages which appear particularly apposite to a *Barder* application:

a. '*The question is not whether a future event is literally incapable of being imagined. The capacity of homo sapiens to imagine fictive things is vast. The question is posed by the court standing retrospectively in the shoes of the actors and asking itself whether the then future, but by now past, event could reasonably have been predicted*'.

b. *As to foreseeability in the context of an event 'where at the time of the order a thing is known and assumed but in fact later eventuates to an extent that was not expected. These are the "known unknown" cases, to use the celebrated language of Secretary Rumsfeld. Plainly it is very difficult to satisfy the test of unforeseeability in such a case*'.

Mostyn J in *DB v DLJ* further held that the standard in the Family Court for foreseeability must be the same as in the rest of the High Court. Thus, King's Bench Division authorities on remoteness apply.

The assets in *HW v WW* were modest outside a company. There were two properties with combined net equity of £529,422, modest pension provision and limited income on W's behalf. W had vast debts of some £200k, £120k of which related to legal fees.

As above, the deal had included H retaining the family company which had previously been owned 51% by him, 49% by W albeit only for tax reasons; it was H's business in reality. The company was valued at £3,147,400 net and was predicted to give H maintainable income of £348,957 net per annum. The company specialised in printers and copiers; on the face of it plainly vulnerable to circumstances which forced everyone to work from home and drastically sped up a move to paperless working in many fields.

Come the pandemic, H's case was the company's sales had fallen off a cliff and the funding that had been available to fund the share buyback which would raise W's lump sum had been withdrawn. To prove this, H had provided draft accounts, a re-valuation of the company by the company accountant and data from a market specialist as to the state of the market.

The full arguments will not be set out but of note it was submitted on W's behalf that H had failed to particularise a specific event or set of circumstances within the *Barder* criteria and it was further submitted that the Covid-19 pandemic was known to the parties at the time of the settlement.

Similarly the evidence will not be delved into although it is noted as is so often the case with businesses, H was presenting one state of affairs to the court and another (more positive state) to the bank.

As a broad statement of principle, HHJ Kloss was not persuaded that the pandemic amounted to a natural price fluctuation as in *Cornick* and *Myerson*. He held:

> "*The Covid 19 pandemic is an extraordinary event, different in nature and scale, to any similar world event in the lifetime of the parties. This is not an issue of market volatility which is*

> *periodically experienced, neither is it a national issue with predictable localised causes. It is akin to a war, with tentacles spreading across the world. I therefore find that in principle, the Covid 19 pandemic can open the door to a successful Barder claim. Myerson can therefore be distinguished and this case, in principle, could fall within the third category in Cornick.*"

This case however, turned on foreseeability and is of particular interest for that reason. HHJ Kloss was satisfied that the pandemic fell into the expanded definition of 'new event' set out by Thorpe LJ in *Myerson* but did note that because the event was known at the time of the deal, it made determining foreseeability that bit harder.

HHJ Kloss fairly asked himself what exactly it was that H was supposed to foresee. His formulation was whether, as at 12 March 2020, H could reasonably have foreseen a risk that the Covid-19 pandemic might have a significant impact upon the trading position of the company. He was not persuaded that H would have needed to foresee the full extent of the pandemic (which was not known even at the time of the hearing).

HHJ Kloss ultimately concluded the risk to the company was foreseeable. He outlined the global trajectory of events, pointing to British Airways' suspension of flights to and from China as early as 29 January 2020 and concluding H was clearly on notice of significant and developing world events. The FTSE 100 had already fallen, Europe was partly in lockdown.

The test of course is not objective, it is subjective. It is whether H in H's shoes could have foreseen the risk. H was an experienced man of business, his business had an international supply chain including China and the implications of a lockdown on a business selling printers is obvious; indeed paperless working had already been identified as a risk to the business. Ultimately whilst the full extent of the impact of the pandemic was not foreseeable, the general risk was foreseeable and that is all that is required to take the case out of the third category identified by Hale J in *Cornick*.

HHJ Kloss moved on to consider the overall impact on the company in case he was wrong on the categorisation of the event. He was not persuaded the change was fundamental enough to meet the test. He cemented his views by again noting that H chose this structure and if the company had specialised in PPE for example, W would not have been able to apply to increase her award so H should not be able to set aside the order either.

HHJ Kloss did flag in his judgment the potential availability of the *Thwaite* jurisdiction to alter the timing of the lump sums notwithstanding they are a series of lump sums; that jurisdiction will be explored later in this book.

This case is ultimately a helpful indication of what kind of global event might constitute a *Barder* event and not simply be natural price fluctuation of the kind observed in *Myerson*. It is further a helpful distillation of foreseeability; one need not foresee the full extent, but in the same way simply foreseeing the Covid-19 pandemic would not have been enough. It was foreseeing cause and effect, namely foreseeing the risk of a significant impact on the company, with the test applied subjectively.

BT v CU

BT v CU [2021] EWFC 87 rounds off this triumvirate of cases. Whilst the judgment is dated 1 November 2021, the events leading to it pre-date the previous two cases.

As with *FRB v DCA*, this was an imposed order rather than by consent. The four-day trial ended on 10 October 2019 with the order expressed as a series of lump sums, totalling £950k and payable yearly on 1 November, with the first lump sum £150k and the remainder £200k. There was also a pension share and spousal maintenance ordered until the payment of the final lump sum.

As part of the final order, H would retain a business which provided school meals and it was on this basis that the 58/42 split in his favour was justified; the business had non-matrimonial origins and also carried the element of risk.

H applied on 27 April 2020 to set aside parts of the order due to the onset of the pandemic. It was not until 12 January 2021 (pre-*HH v WW*) that an order was made directing a preliminary hearing to consider: (a) is Covid capable of being a *Barder* event and (b) has H established sufficient grounds to set aside the final order.

Mostyn J heard the preliminary hearing. He considered both *Cornick* and *Myerson* and in considering the first question posed for the hearing, he considered that Covid probably was not capable of being a *Barder* event albeit every case is fact specific. He queried whether there was a real difference between a business being devastated by the 2008 financial crisis (i.e. *Myerson*) versus a business being devastated by the pandemic.

Mostyn J analysed the financial evidence produced by H to evidence change and was sceptical about the pessimism of the projections. Even so, the financial impact paled into comparison with the impact on Mr Myerson's company and so if Myerson did not fall into the category of a *Barder* event then this could not either. Pausing there; in *Myerson* such was the impact that the asset split was 105.2% in W's favour by the time of the Court of Appeal hearing, albeit with a potentially fluid asset value being shares in the company. If such a dramatic fall in that case was not sufficient to establish a *Barder* event, it is difficult to see what could constitute a *Barder* event on similar facts, unless there was conclusive evidence that the fall was irreversible and beyond market fluctuation.

Mostyn J further held that even if H was right, he could not accept the financial impact was unforeseeable or that they invalidated a fundamental assumption on which the order was based. He considered a reasonable person in October 2019 would have said there was certainly a chance, which could not sensibly be ignored, that in the next year there would be an economic downturn which would have the effect of reducing turnover and increasing costs. Interestingly, unlike *HW v WW*, no oral evidence was heard on this point of foreseeability and there does not seem to have been the same subjective analysis undertaken by Mostyn J as undertaken by HHJ Kloss there.

Mostyn J considered H's application failed at the first limb. His judgment goes on to consider alternative routes, namely variation of the lump sum order under either the inherent jurisdiction or s.31 Matrimonial Causes Act 1973, as outlined in the previous chapter, or under the *Thwaite* jurisdiction which will be considered later in this book.

CHAPTER SIX

OTHER BARDER EVENTS

As far as possible this book has sought to group the main categories of *Barder* events, or attempts at *Barder* events given the wholesale failure of any Covid-linked application. Invariably a little tidying up in a miscellaneous chapter is required.

This chapter therefore will consider three other events which have formed the basis of *Barder* applications:

a. A change in the law;

b. One party's subsequent cohabitation or remarriage.

c. Subsequent inheritance.

This is by no means an exhaustive categorisation of all the different events individuals over the years have sought to claim are *Barder* events, such as redundancy, but this is a book not an encyclopaedia.

Change in the law

S v S (Ancillary Relief: Consent Order)

Readers will know that 2000 was rather an important year in the world of what was then termed ancillary relief. The House of Lords' judgment in *White v White* [200] 2 FLR 981 changed the way the court approached cases under the Matrimonial Causes Act 1973 in a way which resonates to this day and is probably the reason why the Matrimonial Causes Act

1973 has managed to survive for 50 years, albeit the harbingers of change are now looming on the horizon.

Such was the significance of *White* that in the case of *S v S (Ancillary Relief: Consent Order)* [2002] 1 FLR 1992, W sought to argue that a consent order should be set aside on the basis that the development of the law undermined the fundamental assumptions underlying the consent order. In the alternative she ran that there was a mistake of law which vitiated her consent to the order. That will not be addressed as being beyond the parameters of this book.

The consent order was signed on 7 August 2000 and perfected on 12 September 2000. The appeals in *White* were heard in July 2000 with judgment due in the autumn.

The order provided for W to receive assets of £1.1 million and H to retain over £4 million. The parties had met at university when neither had any assets and the marriage ran for approximately 24 years. By any account were such an application to come before the court today, the starting point would invariably be an equal division.

Bracewell J first considered whether a change in the law can in principle amount to a supervening event which would satisfy the first of Lord Brandon's conditions. Having considered comparable civil law authorities, Bracewell J was satisfied that a change in the law could be a supervening event.

Bracewell J went on to consider whether the change in *White* is such a change that it comes within the meaning of *Barder*. The proposition was resisted by H's counsel on the basis that the statutory framework remained unchanged and that the entire exercise was discretionary. Bracewell J did not agree; he concluded that the change was significant enough to represent a supervening event. She noted the successful appeal of the wife in *Cowan v Cowan* [2001] 2 FLR 192, where a pre-*White* first instance decision was revised in light of *White v White* and in particular 'reasonable requirements' were abandoned.

S v S is therefore authority for the proposition that a change in the law can be a *Barder* event and that *White v White* was a sufficiently seismic shift to amount to a supervening event.

As is so often the case, the appeal rested on foreseeability. Bracewell J devised three propositions:

a. The new event must be a complete change of circumstances and not one arising from a development of facts known or which should have been known at the time of the order. If the possibility of an event occurring was or should have been recognised at the time of the order, and that event duly happened, but on a scale unforeseen, then that will not amount to a qualifying supervening event.

b. Even if the new event did not arise from pre-existing facts it must still be unforeseeable in the sense that it was not envisaged and could not reasonably have been envisaged at the time of making the order.

c. If with diligent inquiry the supervening event could have been ascertained prior to its occurrence then a person who fails to make such inquiry cannot seek to impugn the order.

Unfortunately for W, Bracewell J was satisfied that the development in *White* was not only foreseeable but was an obvious possibility. It was after all well known that the appeal was ongoing and it was expected that the court's approach to the exercise of the section 25 Matrimonial Causes Act 1973 discretion would be thoroughly reviewed. Thus, W's application failed at the foreseeability hurdle, which has morphed into a 1A of Lord Brandon's original 4 conditions.

De Renee v Galbraith-Marten

From considering Bracewell J's judgment in *S v S*, one might be forgiven for concluding that any change in the law is going to be so clearly foreshadowed that it could never be unforeseeable. Such a conclusion can be proven wrong however, by the case of *De Renée v Galbraith-Marten* [2023] EWFC 141. The case did not particularly start out as a *Barder* application but was read as such by Cobb J.

These were long-running proceedings with a complex history (M is the subject of an extended civil restraint order), but for the purposes of this application the relevant dispute was in relation to child maintenance. There had been an order in place from June 2018 made pursuant to M's application under Schedule 1 Children Act 1989.

A variation order was agreed by consent in December 2022 after a hearing before Mostyn J on 4 October 2022, where M was given permission to issue a new Schedule 1 application limited to general maintenance ([2022] EWFC 118). The order provided F's maintenance liability would be calculated by applying the formula appearing in Schedule 1 to the Child Support Act 1991 without applying the £156k cap which is utilised when the Child Maintenance Service applies the formula.

This agreement was in accordance with the orthodoxy promulgated by Mostyn J at the time, traceable back to *GW v RW* [2003] EWHC 611 (Fam) and repeated, albeit with some finessing, right up until his judgment in *James v Seymour* [2023] EWHC 844 (Fam). Readers will no doubt be familiar with the judgment, which stepped away from a pure application of the Child Support Act 1991 formula. In a judgment which makes liberal use of acronyms, Mostyn J came up with an adjusted formula methodology (AFM) to provide the child support starting point (CSSP) in cases where general maintenance was in issue (as opposed to what he terms a Household Expenditure Child Support Award (HECSA)).

F's case thus effectively amounted to a variation on the basis that he had followed Mostyn J's approach in December 2022 only for that approach to change, so now he wanted to follow Mostyn J's revised approach. F's case in fact was that Mostyn J had in effect given an indication at the hearing on 4 October 2022 as to the correct approach and this is reflected in Mostyn J's judgment.

It obviously helped F that the adjusted formula in *James v Seymour* produced a far more reasonable outcome than the pure application of the CSA 1991 formula but at the same time one can sympathise if he had simply followed a judge's indication only for that same judge to change his mind some months later. M obviously opposed F's application.

Cobb J considered the way F presented his case and concluded it was in reality a set aside application on *Barder* grounds. Cobb J set out the law concisely and added to the various judicial gloss on the original Lord Brandon conditions by highlighting that the court's residual jurisdiction even after all the conditions have been satisfied should be exercised in accordance with the overriding objective.

Cobb J then turned to foreseeability, which engages interesting points. Mostyn J's previously accepted orthodoxy had been subject to some challenge. Notably he started to refine the methodology to say it would not apply to HECSA cases (*Collardeau-Fuchs v Fuchs* [2022] EWFC 135) and Moor J attacked the inconsistencies produced by the blanket application of a formula in *CMX v EJX* [2022] EWFC 136. However, both these judgments whilst pre-dating the consent order, post-dated the hearing in October 2022. F whilst a barrister by trade was not a family law barrister and was a litigant in person for the proceedings save for ad hoc advice on a direct access basis. Cobb J had then in March 2023 noted that at best the Mostyn J orthodoxy was a guideline for a starting point only (*Re Z (No 4)(Schedule 1 award)* [2023] EWFC 25), which obviously significantly post-dated the consent order.

Cobb J was satisfied that the change in approach from Mostyn J did invalidate the fundamental assumption on which the consent order was made, which had to be right because F's case was that he simply was willing to do whatever Mostyn J said should happen. Cobb J was further satisfied that the change was not foreseeable at the time of the consent order. There was no issue with the remaining *Barder* conditions.

This will remain an exceptional basis to challenge an order on a *Barder* basis and it will be an unusual legal point on which there has been consistent judicial views for 20 years, only to change in an unforeseen way.

Cohabitation and remarriage

Cook v Cook

When is cohabitation sufficient to overturn a consent order? This question was considered by the Court of Appeal in *Cook v Cook* [1988] 1 FLR 521, coming hot on the heels of the House of Lords' judgment in *Barder*.

In a set of facts worthy of a soap opera, after 10 years of marriage H and W became friendly with another married couple (Mr and Mrs M). They subsequently swapped partners; H left the family home to live with Mrs M. Mr and Mrs M separated and their property was sold. H and Mrs M bought a new house together. However, W and Mr M's relationship *appeared* to have cooled. W obtained Decree Absolute in June 1986 and continued to live in the family home with the children. In August 1986 she resumed a relationship with Mr M with a degree of cohabitation and on 15 December 1986 consent order was agreed. This provided amongst other things for a transfer of the family home to W in full and final settlement of all her claims.

H was aware of the renewed relationship with Mr M but W failed to declare her intention to cohabit with Mr M in the court form (Form 91) which was the predecessor to today's Form D81. Shortly after the consent order, H found out W had been inaccurate as to her intentions to cohabit and he immediately made an application to appeal on the basis that W's cohabitation invalidated the basis of the order. H's application for permission to appeal out of time was allowed but his application to rehear the financial remedy application in light of the new events was dismissed, on the basis that the change would have made no difference to the order.

H appealed to the Court of Appeal. Neill LJ's judgment of course referred to *Barder* but also referred to the similarly recent decision of *Livesey v Jenkins* [1985] FLR 813, authority for orders being set aside where there was non-disclosure. In a parallel with *Barder*, Lord Brandon in *Livesey* also commented that simple non-disclosure is not enough, it has to lead the court to make an order which is substantially different from the order which it would have made if such disclosure had taken place.

At the first hearing after the consent order, there was a difficulty in the case run by W. On the one hand it appeared to be said there was no significant change of circumstances after the consent order, as the relationship with Mr M had already been going on, but at the same time she was not dishonest in Form 91. It appeared a contradiction. If there had been a change such that she was not dishonest then of course the cohabitee's resources do become relevant and would at least suggest a re-evaluation of the figures.

As with so many of these cases, it really comes back to foreseeability albeit that element of the *Barder* test had not been so fully developed in 1987. Ultimately Neill LJ was persuaded that there was not really a change, the relationship was ongoing and H knew full well about it; this rather leaves to one side potential dishonesty on a court form but considering the *Barder* test, it is hard to say the development was unforeseeable. Considering non-disclosure, whilst there was potential dishonesty on the court form, H knew full well about the relationship and the prospect of cohabitation was hardly impossible. Similarly, Neill LJ acknowledged the submission that the court re-hearing the case would not make a different order in the context of the limits imposed on an appellate court interfering with a first instance judge's discretion.

It is acknowledged in Neill LJ's judgment that at first blush, if the judge concluded there has been a change of circumstance, then the judge ought to have gone on to say that the figures needed to be looked at all over again. It is far from a statement of principle but it does suggest that there is the notional possibility that subsequent cohabitation might in principle be able to satisfy the first condition of Lord Brandon's *Barder* criteria, if the cohabitee had resources such that it would make a real difference to the outcome. At the same, proximity to the court order will be essential and cohabitation that is sufficiently proximate to an order will inevitably engage foreseeability arguments.

Chaudhuri v Chaudhuri

Taking matters one step further is the case of *Chaudhuri v Chaudhuri* [1992] 2 FLR 73.

The parties' marriage broke down in 1984, one year after the birth of their second child. H left the family home and to use what now seems like prehistoric language, both parents were awarded joint custody of the children with care and control to W.

The financial remedies application came before the court in February 1988 and centred around the family home; H sought a sale, W sought to retain it with the children. The order was appealed but the basic structure survived before the President in May 1988; H received a lump sum from which he was to pay the mortgage on the house and then he received a 25% charge on the property (an ultimate 60/40 split in W's favour), until the older child finished full-time education, W's death or remarriage or permanent cohabitation, whichever event was first. The order, including on appeal, was influenced by W's clear evidence that she needed to retain the property to provide a home for the children.

The house was transferred to W in July 1988 and 11 months later, in June 1989, W's solicitors informed H that W intended to remarry and would be moving to Chester. The eldest child moved to live with H, the youngest child went with W.

H sought to appeal the order out of time, on the basis of a fundamental change in circumstances and in the alternative non-disclosure of a joint bank account held with another man at the time of the appeal hearing. His application was made in January 1990, partly delayed due to a need to secure legal aid funding.

Before Balcombe LJ, the non-disclosure ground was given short shrift; again the consideration is what difference would it have made to the order. As for the *Barder* point and the joint bank account, its only relevance was the extent of the relationship with the man who H was fully aware was a frequent visitor to the family home.

No issue was taken with the timing of H bringing the application, despite a delay of some 6 months after the material event.

The clear difficulty faced by H was that the order specifically contemplated W's remarriage, as remarriage was a term for the crystallisation of the charge and consequent realisation of his remaining share in the equity. It can hardly be said that W's remarriage invalidated the fundamental assumptions underlying the order. Maybe armed with the knowledge, the court may have ordered an immediate sale but then the equity division might have been different.

Balcombe LJ also considered that there had been sufficient time since the original order (some 13 months) that permission to grant leave to appeal out of time could not be given, albeit the time was described as near the borderline.

It is fair to say Balcombe LJ expressed sympathy with the application:

> "*There were, it seemed to me, grounds which entitled the husband to make this application. It is always disturbing, to put it no higher, when one sees a case argued at first instance on a*

> *certain basis and yet, within a comparatively short period of time, events happening which change that basis. But nevertheless, once one makes orders of the clean break type, which involve a once-for-all division of the matrimonial assets, it is inevitable that, in some cases, circumstances will change, and, of course, the obvious possibility is, as happened here, one or both of the parties remarrying, with all the consequential changes that that will involve.*"

This is a helpful reminder of the potency of the clean break; a simple change will not be enough to unravel. The application therefore failed on the first two of the Lord Brandon conditions, the first condition of course incorporating the issue of foreseeability which has been much developed.

Does this case suggest that waiting 12 months before remarrying gives adequate protection? It would be a stretch to draw such a principle. Ultimately H's application failed because the order specifically provided for the eventuality he said was so significant it changed the order. Had the law been more developed at this stage, the judgment would also no doubt have considered the foreseeability of W remarrying, albeit where an order is imposed rather than by consent, it would be harder to hold this against H. He after all at first instance sought an immediate sale.

Can we extract from the case a general principle that remarriage cannot be a *Barder* event? Again that would be a stretch. At the same time, it would be an unusual set of facts indeed whereby a remarriage was not foreseeable, happened sufficiently proximate to the order and was so significant that it invalidated the fundamental assumptions underlying the order.

Inheritance

In *Critchell v Critchell* [2016] 1 FLR 400, H's father died within a month of the consent order, leaving him £180k and writing off an £85k loan. Was this a *Barder* event?

The parties had been married for 9 years with two children. On separation, H borrowed £85k from his father to purchase a house, otherwise the only asset of the marriage was the family home with equity of £175k. Both parties had limited incomes.

After an FDR, H and W entered into a consent order which provided for the family home to be transferred to W on a Mesher basis, subject to the mortgage which she would pay, and a charge over the house in H's favour equivalent to 45% of the net proceeds of sale. The charge had the conventional triggers of youngest child turning 18/finishing secondary education, W's death, remarriage or cohabitation or sale of the property.

When H's father passed away (accepted to be completely unforeseen), leaving the inheritance, W appealed under *Barder* claiming the inheritance undermined the basis of the consent order. HHJ Wright agreed and extinguished H's charge on the house completely. H appealed but found little sympathy with Black LJ who dismissed his appeal.

The familiar conditions from Lord Brandon's judgment form the bedrock of the legal analysis and much discussion focused on the first condition; does the inheritance undermine the fundamental assumptions underlying the consent order?

The analysis must be seen in context; this was a typical needs case, bearing in mind the ultimate outcome was a Mesher order. Needs are an elastic concept and will be dictated by how much money there is available to the parties. Whilst inheritance is of course a non-matrimonial asset, it can be drawn upon if needs demand it.

The premise for H's charge on the family home was that he would, in the future, be able to discharge the loan he had taken from his father to purchase his new property. That was H's 'need'. When his father passed away and H's debt was written off, that need went away. Black LJ focused on this more than the scale of the inheritance (she had been taken to *Cornick* but did not consider it overly relevant). She held:

> "*To my mind, this represented a change in the basis, or fundamental assumption, upon which the consent order had been made. It was not so much that the value of the parties' assets had gone up but rather that there had been a fundamental change in the needs for which provision had to be made.*"

There is no mention of the application of the sharing principle or the delineation between matrimonial and non-matrimonial property. It was argued on H's behalf that the Mesher order properly met W's needs during the children's minority but perhaps it could have been further argued that it also ensured that the sharing principle was fairly applied with H's inheritance to be ring-fenced. Ultimately the case seems to have been deemed such a needs case that the source of the assets did not matter and H should not have any of the marital assets at all. Some readers may have a degree of difficulty with this approach.

Nonetheless, this case clearly demonstrates that an unforeseen windfall post-order can be sufficient to justify a *Barder* application. It will not be every case (that is made very clear by Black LJ in her closing remarks), but one can see that in a needs case that was so tight that the Mesher structure had to be used, where H's charge was specifically linked to a liability which was then almost immediately written off, the change was sufficient. It remains the case from Black LJ's judgment that it is the assumptions underlying the order which matter rather than necessarily the quantum of any subsequent windfall. She also went to pains to make clear at the end of her judgment that nothing she said should be seen as extending the *Barder* jurisprudence which had rightly been applied restrictively over the years since *Barder*.

CHAPTER SEVEN

THE THWAITE JURISDICTION

If it looks like a *Barder* application and sounds like a *Barder* application, is it a *Barder* application? Possibly, but it might just be an application under the *Thwaite* jurisdiction.

It should be stated at the outset that unlike *Barder*, which benefits from clear judicial consistency in terms of the correct approach and the resultant impact on the court's powers, there is judicial conflict at High Court level as to the extent to which the *Thwaite* jurisdiction genuinely exists, certainly in its most extreme form. The main detractor of the jurisdiction, Mostyn J, has now retired and it remains to be seen whether anyone else will take up the baton for the Court of Appeal to rule on.

Nevertheless, in a non-Mostyn J interpretation of the *Thwaite* jurisdiction, this may just provide an alternative argument to run instead of, or alongside, a *Barder* application. Eager readers may recall that HHJ Kloss speculated as much in *HW v WW* [2021] EWFC B20, but neither party invited him to use that jurisdiction.

Thwaite v Thwaite

The originating authority is of course *Thwaite v Thwaite* (1981) 2 FLR 280, a decision of the Court of Appeal. This pre-dates *Barder* by some 6 years.

The parties were married from 1967 to 1976, in that time they had three children. On separation W went to live with another man in Australia and the children eventually joined her. The parties divorced in 1977 in

England and W applied for a financial remedy. On 30 April 1979, the parties entered into a consent order in which W undertook to make a home for the children in England and arrange for them to attend a local school. On the strength of W's undertaking, H was to transfer his interest in the family home to W, with W's claims otherwise dismissed and child periodical payments. The order included the now standard wording of "liberty to apply".

The children returned to England in May 1979 but there was a delay in completing the conveyance of the family home. On 27 August, before the conveyance had been completed, W and the children returned to Australia to join W's new partner.

H, understandably, refused to complete the transfer and applied for a variation. W cross-applied for enforcement. At first instance, H's application was refused and the order enforced. H appealed the refusal and at the same time obtained leave to appeal out of time for the original consent order.

On appeal, H's appeal against the enforcement order succeeded, but he failed in his attempt to vary the order. His attempt to appeal the consent order also failed for want of jurisdiction; again this was pre-*Barder*. The judge did however use the liberty to apply provision to make nominal periodical payments to W, a lump sum of £1,000 and an increase in the child periodical payments, on the basis that he was not enforcing the transfer. W appealed.

The Court of Appeal held in summary (and these are the *Thwaite* principles relied upon in subsequent applications):

a. Where an order is still executory (i.e. it has not been fully complied with) and a party applies to enforce it, the court may refuse to enforce it if it would be inequitable to do so.

b. The judge did have jurisdiction to hear an appeal from the consent order, it was on the basis of fresh evidence, being W

> having no settled intention to remain in England, thus undermining the original basis of the order. The judge was therefore able to make new orders but this was not under liberty to apply, it was due to the fact that W's claim remained open as the conveyance had never been executed.

The conveyance had not been completed, so the order was executory. That opened the door to these two principles, the latter of which closely resembles a *Barder* application albeit without so many preconditions. All that the Court of Appeal set out on the latter point is:

> "*The learned judge was wrong in thinking that he had no jurisdiction to hear an appeal from the consent order in the circumstances of this case. In our judgment he had jurisdiction to set it aside on the basis of the fresh evidence, not available on April 30, 1979, as to the wife's intention to make a home for herself and the children at 19 Howells Road. The order was based on the belief that she had a settled intention to do so; the fresh evidence proved, as the judge found, that she had no such settled intention. But he was in error in holding that he had jurisdiction to do this under the liberty to apply reserved by the order of April 30, 1979.*"

Fresh evidence undermined the basis of the order. It does not say fundamental basis or assumptions as in the *Barder* test and undoubtedly has to be seen as couched in softer terms.

A few years later when the appeal in *Barder* came before the House of Lords, the only mention of *Thwaite* is in support of the familiar proposition that the provisions of any consent order derive their effect from the order, not the agreement, because of the court's overriding jurisdiction to approve any consent order. As will be seen below, Mostyn J considered that meant the House of Lords did not endorse the approach in *Thwaite*.

The Mostyn J perspective

There are two key judgments which set out Mostyn J's scepticism as to the very existence of the *Thwaite* jurisdiction. As set out at this start of this chapter, this is not a view shared by his colleagues at the High Court bench or indeed in the Court of Appeal. His perspective is addressed here because Mostyn J's influence on the development of case law should not be understated and inevitably a Court of Appeal decision is awaited which will consider the competing arguments.

In the same year as Roberts J's decision in *US v SR* (below) came Mostyn J's judgment in *SR v HR* [2018] EWHC 606 (Fam). A consent order provided for property adjustment orders for 3 properties in Carmarthen, with a further consent order finessing the arrangements without altering the substance. They were not implemented, thus the parties returned to court and there was an implementation order. W appealed the implementation order and the Circuit Judge gave her permission to appeal; it was unclear before Mostyn J what the extent of the permission was, namely whether she also had permission to appeal the original consent orders.

The Circuit Judge, HHJ Sharpe, on hearing the appeal decided to deal with the case anew rather than exercising his appeal powers. He considered able to do this on the basis that the orders remained executory. He duly made an entirely new order which had the effect of moving £46k from H to W. Just before the new order was made, H was made bankrupt. H duly appealed the new order and the trustee in bankruptcy intervened.

HHJ Sharpe's reasoning for his jurisdiction is recorded in a recital:

> "*the court may consider the order and refuse to enforce the order if it is inequitable to do so. Where such an outcome is determined it is open to the court to determine the matter afresh.*"

This appears to blur the lines between the two Thwaite principles. Where an order is executory, the court can refuse to enforce it if it would be unfair to do so. That situation however, does not inexorably lead to the court being able to determine it afresh. There is still in the latter case a *Barder*-ish requirement to adduce fresh evidence which undermines the basis of the original order.

Mostyn J observed as much and cited directly from *Thwaite*. Having considered the authorities cited in support in *Thwaite*, he noted that they provide scant support for the proposition that the court can refuse to enforce a consent order and did not consider they provided any support for the ability to make a new order. He held: "*I think that any application under the principle in Thwaite should be approached extremely cautiously and conservatively.*"

At this stage Mostyn J acknowledged the possibility of not enforcing an order but did not appear to accept that there was jurisdiction to make a new order. He therefore set aside the new order of HHJ Sharpe for want of jurisdiction and restored the original consent orders.

Mostyn J approached the issue again in the previously referenced case of *BT v CU* [2021] EWFC 87. In the three years since *SR v HR*, his views had hardened.

He considered the ability to make new orders on the basis of fresh evidence had clearly been overtaken by *Barder*, as it would be wrong to have a stricter test under *Barder* than *Thwaite*.

As to the ability to refuse to enforce an order, Mostyn J noted that *Thwaite* was cited to the House of Lords in *Barder* and is referenced only in relation to the effect of a consent order as above. Mostyn J thus concluded:

> "*it must be strongly emphasised that in Barder itself, Lord Brandon observed at page 10 that the order under appeal was executory. Yet, fully aware of the decision in Thwaite, the*

> *Committee did not decide the case by reference to that doctrine. I agree with Ms Kisser that the Committee must be taken as having impliedly rejected this route as a legitimate source of relief.*"

Mostyn J again considered the authorities cited in *Thwaite* as he did in *SR v HR*. He again confirmed that he considered at best *Thwaite* to be authority for a jurisdiction to refuse to enforce an order, but not to make a fresh order.

He went on to consider the issue of a refusal to enforce, drawing an analogy with the court's jurisdiction to order a stay, in effect a permanent stay. Having considered authorities which considered CPR r.40.8A which allows the civil court to grant a stay, Mostyn J held:

> "*I would go further than Morgan J and hold that a permanent stay could only be lawfully ordered under this rule, or under FPR 4.1(3)(g), if the Barder test is fully satisfied. Were it otherwise, there would exist a means of obtaining relief indistinguishable from that in Barder but without having to satisfy the rigour of the Barder conditions.*"

On Mostyn J's analysis therefore, the only relevance of the *Thwaite* jurisdiction is an ability to refuse to enforce an executory order but rather than being simply if it would be unfair to do so, it must be on *Barder* levels, i.e. a new event which fundamentally undermines the assumptions on which the order was based. This analysis is a significant departure from the *dicta* of Ormrod LJ in *Thwaite* and the authorities to which he referred in that case, which included a judgment of Denning MR.

<u>The current reigning approach?</u>

There is a line of authority which runs contrary to Mostyn J's views. These all post-date *Barder* and stretch up to the Court of Appeal, albeit in a decision refusing permission to appeal which has not been certified, so not technically binding.

The first such case is a decision of Munby J in *L v L* [2006] EWHC 956 (Fam), which concerned a consent order. Munby J's cynicism about H's application is encapsulated in the second sentence of his judgment: "*The husband repents of his generosity to his wife and now seeks to escape from the order to which he consented. The issue before me is whether he can.*"

The parties separated in February 2004, with H leaving the house between 13-21 February. They met on 22 February 2004 in a hotel to discuss their finances and reached an agreement. Solicitors were instructed afterwards. Between solicitors, a final consent order was agreed on 28 September 2004.

H signed Form M1 (predecessor to Form D81) setting out his asset position, as did W a few days later. H therefore signed his Form M1, and the consent order, without sight of W's signed Form M1 and indeed there was doubt as to whether he had even seen a draft.

The consent order included an astonishing undertaking for periodical payments payable to W by H if her net household income (including any income of a cohabitee or spouse) fell below £75k; the quantum was the difference between her actual income and £75k on a net basis, payable for their joint lives with no clause for remarriage or cohabitation.

In her Form M1 W omitted any reference to her bonus, which subsequently proved to be huge; her basic salary in 2004-5 was £135k but total gross income inclusive of bonus was £853,565.

The order was duly sealed in October 2004 as box work. A few months later, in February 2005, W informed H she was giving up work and asked for a direct debit for her maintenance. H then contacted his solicitors to see if he could change the order. H had a conference with leading counsel then changed solicitors. He made the following applications:

1. Application in Form A for an order for periodical payments to W and discharge of his undertaking to pay periodical payments.

2. Appeal against the consent order to include permission to appeal out of time.

3. Application under Part 8 CPR to set aside the consent order.

4. Application in the Family Division to set aside the order.

In other words he threw everything he possibly could at the order, including throwing his previous solicitors under the bus. His case as cited from his witness statement amounted to feeling he was under pressure and that he felt guilty for his chief role in the breakdown of the marriage. The judgment itself is extremely detailed and cannot even be summarised in full; much is devoted to analysis of what led to the agreement including discussions between H and his former solicitors.

Munby J considered 5 scenarios in which he might be able to trigger a review of a consent order. *Barder* of course was in there but entirely separately was *Thwaite*: "*if the terms of the order remain executory*".

As a side note, this case is authority for the proposition that bad legal advice cannot be a ground or justification for setting aside a consent order.

Munby J moved on to consider the court's ability to release or modify an undertaking. On this he cited *Mid Suffolk District Council v Clarke* [2006] EWCA Civ 71 and drew the principle that: "*the court can modify or release an undertaking contained in a final order only if (i) it is just to do so and (ii) there has been a "significant change of circumstances"*."

Unlike Mostyn J, Munby J was satisfied that the *Thwaite* jurisdiction existed and he cited a *Barder* authority, *Benson v Benson (deceased)* [1996] 1 FLR 692, in which Bracewell J held: "*the judge has an inherent jurisdiction to make a fresh order for ancillary relief where the original order remains executory if the basis upon which it was made has fundamentally altered.*"

However, Munby J was clear this did not give rise to an unfettered jurisdiction. He considered that a similar principle to discharging an undertaking must apply when the court is being invited not to enforce an executory order under the *Thwaite* jurisdiction. He noted an apparent conflict; is a significant change of circumstances enough or is a *Barder*-style event required as in *Benson*. He declined to resolve it.

The actual applications before Munby J were W's applications to strike out H's various applications. The analysis of the judgment can therefore stop here. H could not establish a case under *Thwaite* because there had not been any material change in circumstances since the consent order. The only change was that W had stopped working thus triggering H's undertaking, but that clearly does not pass the significance test let alone a *Barder* test. As is fairly obvious however, H was permitted to run a variation case under s.31 Matrimonial Causes Act 1973.

Next up is the permission to appeal hearing in *Bezeliansky v Bezelianskaya* [2016] EWCA Civ 76. Again it should be noted this is a permission to appeal judgment only so is not binding, albeit plainly it would be extremely persuasive, it being a panel of three Court of Appeal judges hearing the matter with the lead judgment given by the future President of the Family Division, McFarlane LJ.

The case concerned a consent order dated 9 January 2013, made by Holman J. Amongst other provisions it provided for a Monaco and a Moscow property to be transferred to W and a Paris property to be held by H (it was owned through a company).

On 2 March 2015, the matter came before Moor J, with total non-compliance with the consent order. Moor J made an order which substantially varied the capital provision in the original order. He changed it so that H would retain the Moscow property and the shares in the company holding the Paris property would be transferred to W, on the basis the property would be sold and the net proceeds held to the order of the court save for various distributions to W in satisfaction of H's failure to comply with orders.

Alongside appeals against committal orders, H appealed Moor J's order to the Court of Appeal, albeit he did not himself attend the hearing.

Moor J was satisfied that he had jurisdiction to do what he did under the *Thwaite* jurisdiction. Quite clearly this goes beyond simply not enforcing an order, Moor J fundamentally set aside the original order and substituted a new one.

H submitted that *Thwaite* did not give jurisdiction to vary the terms of the consent order, only to refuse to enforce a consent order. The Court of Appeal did not agree and noted H's selective citation of the headnote from the law report of *Thwaite*. McFarlane LJ went on to set out the remainder of the headnote which confirmed there was jurisdiction to set aside the consent order on the basis of fresh evidence because the order was executory.

McFarlane LJ therefore considered that Moor J had been entitled to exercise the full *Thwaite* jurisdiction.

H also relied upon *L v L*:

> "*The appellant submits that the test for setting aside a consent order drawn from Munby J's judgment in L v L at paragraph 67, namely that it would be inequitable to do otherwise in the light of a significant change in circumstances, is a constant across the board in relation to each of the various mechanisms available by which a consent order may be varied or set aside;*

> *the fact that a particular order may be "executory" does not alter or water-down that position."*

McFarlane LJ responded: "*Insofar as it may be relevant, I disagree with that submission.*" His view on the correct test to be applied for a *Thwaite* application was (emphasis added):

> "*With respect to cases where there is an undertaking or an order that is still executory the approach to determining whether or not to set aside or vary the order is, as the appellant submits, based upon it being inequitable to hold to the terms of the original order in the light of a significant change of circumstances. Given that this is a case about an executory order, it is not necessary to engage any further with the Appellant's wider submission regarding the test where the jurisdiction may arise in other circumstances. In any event I agree with Mr Chamberlayne that the circumstances justifying intervention are likely to be met where an order remain executory as a result of one party frustrating its implementation.*"

Pausing there; in McFarlane LJ's view, frustration of an order would be sufficient to exercise the full *Thwaite* jurisdiction. This very much fits with the 'inequitable' consideration rather than a *Barder*-style analysis.

H's application for permission to appeal was dismissed but there can be no question that this judgment represents a significant review both of *Thwaite* and the latest authority, namely *L v L*. It supports far more an analysis that a significant change of circumstances is required, rather than a *Barder* event.

In the same year as *SR v HR*, Roberts J heard the case of *US v SR* [2018] EWHC 3207 (Fam). In what is a familiar tale, this was another case of long-running litigation.

The original order in question was made by Roberts J on 1 May 2015, but this order was only made after she handed down judgment on 25

July 2014. Between judgment and order, W moved from England to Moscow with the parties' youngest child with the intention of renting out the FMH. H thus sought to reopen matters using the court's jurisdiction from *Re Barrell Enterprises* [1972] 3 All ER 631, with the order yet to be perfected.

The basis for H's application was simple enough; if W had told the court that within a month of judgment she would be moving to Russia, he would have sought the sale or transfer of the family home which was the only property in England & Wales. H therefore sought to retain the family home and he would deduct the net equity from any sums he was due to receive from the sale of another property.

Roberts J reflected the application by introducing various default measures if the other property was not sold, in particular H retaining the English property. That was May 2015, unfortunately the litigation did not end there. The facts are too convoluted to set out but can be summarised as a war of attrition, chequered by W's non-compliance with sale of foreign properties. Both parties' financial positions were eroded as a result.

For the purposes of this judgment and relevance to this book, H was seeking a sale of the family home within the scheme of the original judgment on the basis that the court had jurisdiction to do so either through *Thwaite* or through s.24A Matrimonial Causes Act 1973 (the court can make an order for sale upon the making of a lump sum order or at any time thereafter).

There could be no question that the order remained executory, that was the entire problem after all. Roberts J took her lead from *Bezeliansky*, referring to the judgment and McFarlane LJ's analysis of *L v L*. Roberts J's decision came just after Mostyn J's judgment in *SR v HR*. She noted that *SR v HR* does not refer to *Bezeliansky* nor, perhaps more importantly, does it refer to *L v L*.

Her view was that Munby J's judgment in *L v L* was consistent with the cautious and conservative approach urged by Mostyn J in *SR v HR*. She took from *L v L* the test approved by McFarlane LJ in *Bezeliansky*, namely: "*the essence of the jurisdiction is that "it would be inequitable not to [vary its terms] because of or in the light of some significant change in the circumstances since the order was made".*"

She sought to incorporate Mostyn J's comments in her approach, however:

> "*I accept, following SR v HR, that any such revision must be contained and, so far as possible, should reflect the underlying intention of the original extraction route embodied in the 2015 mainframe order. That is a jurisdiction which I am exercising with the consent of both parties although I do not need such consent in order to exercise it. It is a jurisdiction which flows both from the Thwaite principle (contained, as explained above) and from the jurisdiction conferred on the court pursuant to the FPR 2010.*"

Thus whilst Roberts J did revise the original order, she did so as consistently as possible with the original. She ordered that the family home be sold and cross-checked her revised outcome against the remaining available assets. She applied the needs principle afresh, ultimately sanctioning an overall 52.5% split in H's favour, not quite as high as the original split but as far as possible to reflect needs.

This case is helpful not just for how it favours the *Bezeliansky* approach instead of Mostyn J's approach, albeit with some incorporation of caution, but also for illustrating how the resultant redistributive exercise had to be undertaken. An effective *de novo* review of the circumstances as they stood at that latest date was undertaken. A last point of interest is that there was no order as to costs for the hearing, perhaps reflective of the destructive role played by both parties at different times over the course of the mammoth litigation.

The last case considered in this section is the judgment of Lieven J in *Kicinski v Pardi* [2021] EWHC 499 (Fam), an appeal from a first instance decision of Recorder Allen QC.

Rather than significantly developing the legal field of *Thwaite*, this is another judgment which follows the approach in *Bezeliansky* and *US v SR*. Lieven J considered that whilst *Bezeliansky* was not technically binding on her, it carried "*the very greatest weight*". At paragraphs 25-33 Lieven J summarises the law. In relation to the Mostyn J judgment in *SR v HR*, Lieven J noted:

> "*Mostyn J sought to place further constraints upon the use of the Thwaite jurisdiction and said it should be approached "extremely cautiously and conservatively". However, as Recorder Allen QC said at J44 in the present case, neither party has placed great weight on this authority, particularly as it is to some degree out of step with the Court of Appeal decision in Bezeliansky.*"

The facts of the case demonstrate an interesting (attempted) use of the *Thwaite* jurisdiction. During the final hearing in financial remedy proceedings, indeed on the last day, the parties settled and drew up an agreement in a *Rose* order. The key term for these purposes was that W was to retain £1.6m of funds in a Swiss bank account and H was to receive the remainder. When the drafting of the order became contentious, W applied under *Thwaite* to vary the terms requiring H to give her and her solicitors an indemnity against any liability to the law firm Withers arising out of possible proceedings brought by H's aunt and uncle (there had been satellite litigation in Italy). At first instance, Recorder Allen QC considered that whilst the order was executory, there had been no material change of circumstances and it would not be inequitable to hold W to the terms of the *Rose* order. W appealed.

W's appeal was allowed. Recorder Allen QC had got the law right, but he had misinterpreted the facts, in essence. The facts are detailed and concern satellite claims by H's aunt and uncle but in essence Lieven J was persuaded that come July 2020, W was in a very materially different position to that which she had agreed to in October 2019. She entered into the agreement assuming all claims of all kinds would be settled but H's aunt and uncle did not in fact withdraw all their disputes.

Lieven J considered it would be inequitable to leave W exposed to a contingent liability in circumstances where the settlement included a clean break. It is perhaps noteworthy as well that the triggering of the indemnity was arguably in H's control; it would after all be his aunt and uncle who would sue Withers thus triggering the indemnity. Being aware of the indemnity, they may opt not to do so and Lieven J had regard to the closely intertwined financial relationship in this regard.

The facts also demonstrate how the *Thwaite* test is truly different to the *Barder* test. This is underscored by Lieven J's conclusions at §51:

> *"In any event, it is not part of the Thwaite tests that the significant change which triggers the jurisdiction must be wholly unforeseen. It would not, in my view, make sense for such an additional requirement to be imposed. It may be, particularly in this area of litigation, that it is foreseeable that one party to the agreed order will seek to renege upon it before it is executed. That does not mean that the change that then occurs is not significant even if to some degree foreseeable. It might well on the facts have been not wholly unexpected that Mrs Thwaite or Mr Bezeliansky would have reneged on part of their respective agreements. The courts have not sought to delve into that issue before applying the Thwaite jurisdiction."*

The change must be significant and there must be unfairness, but the foreseeability criterion which has been built into the *Barder* test has not been so replicated in the *Thwaite* line of authority.

All these cases were considered by Mostyn J in *BT v CU* who pithily commented that he did not agree and that they seemed to conflict with *Barder*. This approach presupposes that *Barder*, in not expressly considering *Thwaite*, can be seen as impliedly rejecting it. The danger with reading implications into the House of Lords'/Supreme Court's judgments was exposed very recently in *Potanina v Potanin* [2024] UKSC 3. In *Potanina*, previous accepted orthodoxy in relation to applications for permission to apply under Part III Matrimonial Family Proceedings Act 1984 based on an understanding of the Supreme Court's judgment in *Agbaje v Agbaje* [2010] UKSC 13 was held to be wrong and a misinterpretation.

Therefore, the question mark in the heading is used purely because of the conflict at first instance level. The weight of authority is currently in favour of the *Thwaite* jurisdiction and undoubtedly Mostyn J's judgments have to be seen as outliers. Whilst a significant influence on the development of the law, Mostyn J's views for example on the starting point for anonymity of reported decisions in the ongoing transparency debate were not adopted as the starting point in the Farquhar report.

The way in particular that Recorder Allen QC then Lieven J dealt with Mostyn J's outlier in *Kicinski v Pardi* is perhaps illustrative of the mainstream approach, namely deferring to the Court of Appeal in *Bezeliansky* rather than the restrictive interpretation urged by Mostyn J.

The final word (for now)

There is one *Thwaite* judgment post-*BT v CU*, the case of *H v W* [2023] EWFC 120, albeit at Circuit Judge level (HHJ Reardon). It concerned a financial remedy order from May 2021 which provided for W to remain in the family home and transfer three properties to H, subject to existing mortgages. The parties in fact agreed for the three properties to be sold instead.

H accused W of delay and issued an application under the *Thwaite* jurisdiction for a further lump sum payment, to compensate him for losses he said he had suffered as a result of W's delay. Other applications were in the mix but for the purposes of this section, it is the *Thwaite* application which is of interest, together with W's cross-application to strike out the *Thwaite* application.

Interestingly there was no real dispute of fact. Like in *Kicinski v Pardi*, this was more about the correct application of the law to the facts. HHJ Reardon considered the state of the law in relation to *Thwaite* in light of *BT v CU*. She considered that *BT v CU* was a paradigm *Barder* case (albeit unsuccessful) and that the *Thwaite* cases can be seen differently. She noted for example that the line of cases which involved frustration of implementation by one party would likely fail the first limb of the *Barder* conditions, noting the possible foreseeability of such actions. It would not be right that litigants in that scenario would be left with no remedy. She again emphasised, as was done by Lieven J in *Kicinski*, that unforeseeability was not a requirement of the *Thwaite* jurisdiction.

HHJ Reardon suggested that *Thwaite* was entirely distinct to *Barder* and suggested its use would be particularly apt where:

> *a.* "*The respondent has culpably acted in such a way as to diminish the value of an asset, or otherwise to frustrate the intention behind the order;*
>
> *b.* *There is a link between the executory nature of the order and the change in circumstances: ie, it is the fact that the order remains executory that has provided the respondent with the opportunity to frustrate it; and*
>
> c. *The applicant might well fail the first limb of the Barder test because the respondent's conduct was foreseeable.*"

As above, Mostyn J has now retired without being able to respond. *H v W* at the time of writing thus remains the final word on *Thwaite*. Having regard to the volume of authority against Mostyn J in this regard, it suggested as things stand, the *Thwaite* jurisdiction remains intact albeit perhaps more susceptible to challenge than the *Barder* jurisdiction.

The broad *Thwaite* jurisdiction must be read in the context of the authorities. The following principles can be outlined:

1. Where an order is still executory and a party applies to enforce it, the court may refuse to enforce it if it would be inequitable to do so.

2. Where an order is still executory, the court may vary its terms if it would be inequitable not to because of or in the light of some significant change in the circumstances since the order was made which undermined the original basis of the order.

a. The significant change does not have to be wholly unforeseeable.

3. So far as possible, any variation to the order should be consistent with the overall objective of the original order.

4. The essence of the jurisdiction is fairness but this does not mean the court approaches the issue with fresh eyes. It adjusts the final order only so far as it would be unfair not to do so.

For self-evident reasons this is different to a *Barder* application and may well provide a slightly softer route into amending an order than a *Barder* application on the right set of facts. The caution exercised by Roberts J in *US v SR* however, is a warning for any litigant who believes they will be able to just tear up an order if there has been a change of circumstances.

A final point of interest; in *H v GH* [2023] EWFC 235, H brought an application to vary the time for payment of a lump sum. H did not seek to stay the payment of the lump sum in reliance on the *Thwaite* jurisdiction. Instead it was brought under the court's inherent jurisdiction and Simon Colton KC (sitting as a deputy High Court Judge) considered he did not have jurisdiction to grant an extension of 2 years some 4 and a half years after the original order. Undoubtedly, the case law relied upon in considering this, particularly *Hamilton v*

Hamilton [2013] EWCA Civ 12 and the lack of a power to extend time for payment for any significant period if the lump sum is not variable under s.31 Matrimonial Causes Act 1973, would make a foundation for an anti-*Thwaite* argument. The difference however is between extending time for payment and actively refusing to enforce in circumstances where it would be unfair to do so because of a significant change in circumstances.

CHAPTER EIGHT

BARDER APPLICATIONS: PROCEDURAL CONSIDERATIONS

An awful lot has been set out in this book, with differing glosses and conditions being applied over the years by different judges. Before setting out the procedural considerations, the various cases need condensing into one definitive Barder test. The following conditions are proposed as being the true *Barder* test as refined over the years:

1. New events (including happenings, developments or occurrences) have occurred since the making of the order which invalidate the basis, or fundamental assumption, upon which the order was made, so that, if leave to appeal out of time were to be given, the appeal would be certain, or very likely, to succeed.

1A. The new event must be unforeseeable:

  a. This is a subjective test.

  b. It is the same test as would be applied in the Kings Bench Division.

  c. If the possibility of an event occurring was or should have been recognised at the time of the order, and that event duly happened but on a scale unforeseen, then that will not amount to a qualifying supervening event.

  d. Even if the new event did not arise from pre-existing facts it must still be unforeseeable in the sense that it was not envisaged and could not reasonably have been envisaged at the time of making the order.

e. If with diligent inquiry the supervening event could have been ascertained prior to its occurrence then a person who fails to make such inquiry cannot seek to impugn the order.

2. The new events should have occurred within a relatively short time of the order having been made. Generally this will less than 1 year after the order but that is not a hard and fast rule.

3. The application for leave to appeal out of time should be made reasonably promptly in the circumstances of the case.

4. The grant of leave to appeal out of time should not prejudice third parties who have acquired, in good faith and for valuable consideration, interests in property which is the subject matter of the relevant order.

5. There is no alternative mainstream relief is available to the applicant which broadly remedies the unfairness caused by the new event.

6. In circumstances where the order being set aside is a consent order, is there any reason why the court should exercise its discretion not to set aside the order. The exercise of the discretion should be in accordance with the overriding objective, namely "*enabling the court to deal with cases justly, having regard to any welfare issues involved*".

In recent years, the procedure for *Barder* applications has been simplified and clarified with the introduction of FPR r.9.9A and PD9A on 3 October 2016. The following procedural points can be taken:

a. An application under *Barder* principles is an application to set aside a financial remedy order, not an appeal.

b. The application must be made to the first instance court.

c. The application must be made in accordance with Part 18 procedure on Form D11, i.e. an application within the existing proceedings. It should be supported by a witness statement and *prima facie* evidence of the change relied upon in support of the application. This will require very careful consideration particularly where the change asserted is economic.

d. The application relies on (iv) of paragraph 13.5 PD9A: "*The grounds on which a financial remedy order may be set aside are and will remain a matter for decisions by judges. The grounds ... (iv) a subsequent event, unforeseen and unforeseeable at the time the order was made, which invalidates the basis on which the order was made.*"

e. The introduction of PD9A in no way softens or affects the test applied in *Barder*: *Akhmedova v Akhmedov and Others* [2021] 1 FLR 667.

Readers will be familiar with the Part 18 procedure. The order sought is not an interim order within the meaning of FPR r.9.7 so at least 7 days' notice is required (but service should be as soon as practicable after it is filed).

In terms of case management, whilst this will be case specific, it is likely that a two-stage approach will be adopted:

1. First stage: is there sufficient evidence to establish that the *Barder* conditions have been met?

2. Second stage: what new order, if any, should be made?

This may happen at one hearing, it may happen over two (or more). The exercise may be split because where for example the accepted change relates to the value a business, the valuation exercise will need to take place again. Where the change is more in principle, for example in a death case, then clearly the matter could be disposed of in one hearing if there is a sufficient time estimate. Of course even before the first stage above, case management may be required for witness statements and the like.

Whether oral evidence is heard at the hearing will again be case specific. If for example, a case turns on the foreseeability of an event at the time of a consent order, it is more likely than not that oral evidence will be required. Other cases may be resolved on submissions and with disclosure for example of the negotiations which led to an agreement, e.g. to divine the purpose of a certain provision.

Lastly, as with any application, one of the most important considerations is costs. A cost/benefit analysis is essential and whilst financial remedy practitioners are used to the protection offered by the no order principle in FPR r.28.3, the judicial trend is strongly moving towards a more proactive costs jurisdiction; consider for example recent guidance from Peel J in *HO v TL* [2023] EWFC 215 (incidentally, superb anonymisation for a case concerning a hotel chain).

Where does a *Barder* application lie? Rule 28.3, the no order as to costs starting point, applies to financial remedy proceedings. Financial remedy proceedings are defined in r.28.3(4)(b). Further on in the rule, r.28.3(9) makes clear that financial remedy proceedings do not include an application under rule 9.9A, i.e. applications to set aside an order.

Therefore if one makes a *Barder* application, there is no protection of the no order as to costs starting point. The approach is the clean sheet, meaning the court has its overall general discretion but will likely adopt a soft starting point of costs follow the event in line with the approach of Butler-Sloss LJ in *Gojkovic v Gojkovic (No 2)* [1991] 2 FLR 233, as confirmed in *Solomon v Solomon* [2013] EWCA Civ 1095 (albeit another permission to appeal hearing).

What of alternatives? The tension in any costs analysis is whether the application is *for* a financial remedy or *about* a financial remedy. The *Barder* case law and frankly common-sense points practitioners towards looking at whether there are any more mainstream alternatives available and the much discussed alternative in the case law is variation of a lump sum order by instalments.

Variation proceedings, whilst specifically marked in PD28A paragraph 4.4 as requiring particularly reasonable negotiation, are financial remedy proceedings per FPR rule 2.3. They are further defined in FPR rule 9.3, as being proceedings brought under s.31 Matrimonial Causes Act 1973 (or the mirror provision in the Civil Partnership Act 2004).

In *H v GH* [2023] EWFC 235, Simon Colton KC sitting as a Deputy High Court Judge was faced with a variation application for the timing of a payment of a lump sum. He considered it to have been brought under the court's inherent jurisdiction under *Masefield v Alexander* [1995] 1 FLR 100, rather than s.31 MCA 1973 (despite the best efforts of H's counsel to pivot on his feet). This is because the application sought an effective stay on the date for payment of one lump sum; it could only fall potentially within s.31(2)(dd) if it was a deferred order for payment of lump sum which included provision for pension rights. As a result he adopted the clean sheet approach rather than the starting point of no order as to costs.

Therefore even if one were to seek to creatively argue that an application say under *Thwaite* in reality amounted to a variation application, because the variation application has not been brought pursuant to the variation provision in 1973 or 2004 Act, it will not come within the no order principle.

All this is to say that where considering an application to set aside under *Barder* or a similar application under *Thwaite*, costs will be live and careful thought will need to be given to prospects of success before taking the matter any further. Numerous judgments referenced in this book have warned of the rarity of a successful *Barder* application and the clear public interest in the finality of litigation.

As a final warning on costs, the case of *L v O* [2024] EWFC 6 relates to a pending final hearing for H's *Barder* application. Alongside an unsuccessful application for a Hadkinson order, W successfully secured an order for security for costs, having satisfied the conditions in FPR rule 20.7, H being out of the jurisdiction. Cobb J was persuaded to exercise his discretion (after much wrangling over whether H was indeed out of the jurisdiction), considering that it was indeed just to make such an order. Cobb J sets out at §44 a repeat of a helpful checklist of the court's approach initially devised by Mostyn J, which is a useful reference point to anyone making such an application. Cobb J was particularly persuaded by the prospective difficulties in enforcing an order and was unimpressed by H's claims an order would stifle his ability to pursue his claim. From W's headline figure of £637,882, Cobb J ordered H pay £480,000 on account, with the risk of his *Barder* application being dismissed summarily in default. This only again reiterates the careful thought required before bringing a *Barder* application.

MORE BOOKS BY LAW BRIEF PUBLISHING

A selection of our other titles available now:-

'A Practical Guide to the Independent School Standards – September 2023 Edition' by Sarah McKimm
'A Practical Guide to Estate Administration and Crypto Assets' by Richard Marshall
'A Practical Guide to Managing GDPR Data Subject Access Requests – Second Edition' by Patrick O'Kane
'A Practical Guide to Parental Alienation in Private and Public Law Children Cases' by Sam King QC & Frankie Shama
'Contested Heritage – Removing Art from Land and Historic Buildings' by Richard Harwood QC, Catherine Dobson, David Sawtell
'The Limits of Separate Legal Personality: When Those Running a Company Can Be Held Personally Liable for Losses Caused to Third Parties Outside of the Company' by Dr Mike Wilkinson
'A Practical Guide to Transgender Law' by Robin Moira White & Nicola Newbegin
'A Practical Guide to 'Stranded Spouses' in Family Law' by Mani Singh Basi
'A Practical Guide to Residential Freehold Conveyancing' by Lorraine Richardson
'A Practical Guide to Pensions on Divorce for Lawyers' by Bryan Scant
'A Practical Guide to Challenging Sham Marriage Allegations in Immigration Law' by Priya Solanki
'A Practical Guide to Digital Communications Evidence in Criminal Law' by Sam Willis
'A Practical Guide to Legal Rights in Scotland' by Sarah-Jane Macdonald
'A Practical Guide to New Build Conveyancing' by Paul Sams & Rebecca East
'A Practical Guide to Defending Barristers in Disciplinary Cases' by Marc Beaumont
'A Practical Guide to Inherited Wealth on Divorce' by Hayley Trim
'A Practical Guide to Practice Direction 12J and Domestic Abuse in Private Law Children Proceedings' by Rebecca Cross & Malvika Jaganmohan

'A Practical Guide to Confiscation and Restraint' by Narita Bahra QC, John Carl Townsend, David Winch
'A Practical Guide to the Law of Forests in Scotland' by Philip Buchan
'A Practical Guide to Health and Medical Cases in Immigration Law' by Rebecca Chapman & Miranda Butler
'A Practical Guide to Bad Character Evidence for Criminal Practitioners by Aparna Rao
'A Practical Guide to Extradition Law post-Brexit' by Myles Grandison et al
'A Practical Guide to Hoarding and Mental Health for Housing Lawyers' by Rachel Coyle
'A Practical Guide to Psychiatric Claims in Personal Injury – 2nd Edition' by Liam Ryan
'Stephens on Contractual Indemnities' by Richard Stephens
'A Practical Guide to the EU Succession Regulation' by Richard Frimston
'A Practical Guide to Solicitor and Client Costs – 2nd Edition' by Robin Dunne
'Constructive Dismissal – Practice Pointers and Principles' by Benjimin Burgher
'A Practical Guide to Religion and Belief Discrimination Claims in the Workplace' by Kashif Ali
'A Practical Guide to the Law of Medical Treatment Decisions' by Ben Troke
'Fundamental Dishonesty and QOCS in Personal Injury Proceedings: Law and Practice' by Jake Rowley
'A Practical Guide to the Law in Relation to School Exclusions' by Charlotte Hadfield & Alice de Coverley
'A Practical Guide to Divorce for the Silver Separators' by Karin Walker
'The Right to be Forgotten – The Law and Practical Issues' by Melissa Stock
'A Practical Guide to Planning Law and Rights of Way in National Parks, the Broads and AONBs' by James Maurici QC, James Neill et al
'A Practical Guide to Election Law' by Tom Tabori
'A Practical Guide to the Law in Relation to Surrogacy' by Andrew Powell
'A Practical Guide to Claims Arising from Fatal Accidents – 2nd Edition' by James Patience
'A Practical Guide to the Ownership of Employee Inventions – From Entitlement to Compensation' by James Tumbridge & Ashley Roughton
'A Practical Guide to Asbestos Claims' by Jonathan Owen & Gareth McAloon

'A Practical Guide to Stamp Duty Land Tax in England and Northern Ireland' by Suzanne O'Hara
'A Practical Guide to the Law of Farming Partnerships' by Philip Whitcomb
'Covid-19, Homeworking and the Law – The Essential Guide to Employment and GDPR Issues' by Forbes Solicitors
'Covid-19 and Criminal Law – The Essential Guide' by Ramya Nagesh
'Covid-19 and Family Law in England and Wales – The Essential Guide' by Safda Mahmood
'A Practical Guide to the Law of Unlawful Eviction and Harassment – 2nd Edition' by Stephanie Lovegrove
'Covid-19, Brexit and the Law of Commercial Leases – The Essential Guide' by Mark Shelton
'A Practical Guide to Costs in Personal Injury Claims – 2nd Edition' by Matthew Hoe
'A Practical Guide to the General Data Protection Regulation (GDPR) – 2nd Edition' by Keith Markham
'Ellis on Credit Hire – Sixth Edition' by Aidan Ellis & Tim Kevan
'A Practical Guide to Working with Litigants in Person and McKenzie Friends in Family Cases' by Stuart Barlow
'Protecting Unregistered Brands: A Practical Guide to the Law of Passing Off' by Lorna Brazell
'A Practical Guide to Secondary Liability and Joint Enterprise Post-Jogee' by Joanne Cecil & James Mehigan
'A Practical Guide to the Pre-Action RTA Claims Protocol for Personal Injury Lawyers' by Antonia Ford
'A Practical Guide to Neighbour Disputes and the Law' by Alexander Walsh
'A Practical Guide to Forfeiture of Leases' by Mark Shelton
'A Practical Guide to Coercive Control for Legal Practitioners and Victims' by Rachel Horman
'A Practical Guide to the Law of Driverless Cars – Second Edition' by Alex Glassbrook, Emma Northey & Scarlett Milligan
'A Practical Guide to TOLATA Claims' by Greg Williams
'A Practical Guide to Elderly Law – 2nd Edition' by Justin Patten
'A Practical Guide to Responding to Housing Disrepair and Unfitness Claims' by Iain Wightwick

'A Practical Guide to the Law of Bullying and Harassment in the Workplace' by Philip Hyland
'How to Be a Freelance Solicitor: A Practical Guide to the SRA-Regulated Freelance Solicitor Model' by Paul Bennett
'A Practical Guide to Prison Injury Claims' by Malcolm Johnson
'A Practical Guide to the Small Claims Track – 2nd Edition' by Dominic Bright
'A Practical Guide to Advising Clients at the Police Station' by Colin Stephen McKeown-Beaumont
'A Practical Guide to Antisocial Behaviour Injunctions' by Iain Wightwick
'Practical Mediation: A Guide for Mediators, Advocates, Advisers, Lawyers, and Students in Civil, Commercial, Business, Property, Workplace, and Employment Cases' by Jonathan Dingle with John Sephton
'The Mini-Pupillage Workbook' by David Boyle
'A Practical Guide to Crofting Law' by Brian Inkster
'A Practical Guide to the Law of Domain Names and Cybersquatting' by Andrew Clemson
'A Practical Guide to the Law of Gender Pay Gap Reporting' by Harini Iyengar
'NHS Whistleblowing and the Law' by Joseph England
'Employment Law and the Gig Economy' by Nigel Mackay & Annie Powell
'A Practical Guide to Noise Induced Hearing Loss (NIHL) Claims' by Andrew Mckie, Ian Skeate, Gareth McAloon
'An Introduction to Beauty Negligence Claims – A Practical Guide for the Personal Injury Practitioner' by Greg Almond
'Intercompany Agreements for Transfer Pricing Compliance' by Paul Sutton
'Zen and the Art of Mediation' by Martin Plowman
'A Practical Guide to the SRA Principles, Individual and Law Firm Codes of Conduct 2019 – What Every Law Firm Needs to Know' by Paul Bennett
'A Practical Guide to Adoption for Family Lawyers' by Graham Pegg
'A Practical Guide to Industrial Disease Claims' by Andrew Mckie & Ian Skeate
'A Practical Guide to Conducting a Sheriff Court Proof' by Andrew Stevenson
'A Practical Guide to Vicarious Liability' by Mariel Irvine
'A Practical Guide to Applications for Landlord's Consent and Variation of Leases' by Mark Shelton
'A Practical Guide to Relief from Sanctions Post-Mitchell and Denton' by Peter Causton

'A Practical Guide to Equity Release for Advisors' by Paul Sams
'A Practical Guide to Financial Services Claims' by Chris Hegarty
'The Law of Houses in Multiple Occupation: A Practical Guide to HMO Proceedings' by Julian Hunt
'Occupiers, Highways and Defective Premises Claims: A Practical Guide Post-Jackson – 2nd Edition' by Andrew Mckie
'A Practical Guide to Financial Ombudsman Service Claims' by Adam Temple & Robert Scrivenor
'A Practical Guide to Running Housing Disrepair and Cavity Wall Claims: 2nd Edition' by Andrew Mckie & Ian Skeate
'A Practical Guide to Holiday Sickness Claims – 2nd Edition' by Andrew Mckie & Ian Skeate
'Arguments and Tactics for Personal Injury and Clinical Negligence Claims' by Dorian Williams
'A Practical Guide to Drone Law' by Rufus Ballaster, Andrew Firman, Eleanor Clot
'A Practical Guide to Compliance for Personal Injury Firms Working With Claims Management Companies' by Paul Bennett
'RTA Allegations of Fraud in a Post-Jackson Era: The Handbook – 2nd Edition' by Andrew Mckie
'RTA Personal Injury Claims: A Practical Guide Post-Jackson' by Andrew Mckie
'On Experts: CPR35 for Lawyers and Experts' by David Boyle
'An Introduction to Personal Injury Law' by David Boyle

These books and more are available to order online direct from the publisher at www.lawbriefpublishing.com, where you can also read free sample chapters. For any queries, contact us on 0844 587 2383 or mail@lawbriefpublishing.com.

Our books are also usually in stock at www.amazon.co.uk with free next day delivery for Prime members, and at good legal bookshops such as Wildy & Sons.

We are regularly launching new books in our series of practical day-to-day practitioners' guides. Visit our website and join our free newsletter to be kept informed and to receive special offers, free chapters, etc.

You can also follow us on Twitter at www.twitter.com/lawbriefpub.

www.ingramcontent.com/pod-product-compliance
Lightning Source LLC
LaVergne TN
LVHW022303200926
848481LV00004B/1197
* 9 7 8 1 9 1 6 6 9 8 3 5 2 *